YOUR KNOWLEDGE HAS VALUE

AF140231

Bibliographic information published by the German National Library:

The German National Library lists this publication in the National Bibliography; detailed bibliographic data are available on the Internet at http://dnb.dnb.de .

Imprint:

Copyright © 2017 GRIN Verlag, Open Publishing GmbH
Print and binding: Books on Demand GmbH, Norderstedt Germany
ISBN: 9783668578548

This book at GRIN:

http://www.grin.com/en/e-book/381269/solving-performance-models-based-on-basic-queueing-theory-formulas

Tatjana Weber

Solving performance models based on basic queueing theory formulas

A study of applicability of queueing theory formulas to queueing networks

GRIN Publishing

GRIN - Your knowledge has value

Since its foundation in 1998, GRIN has specialized in publishing academic texts by students, college teachers and other academics as e-book and printed book. The website www.grin.com is an ideal platform for presenting term papers, final papers, scientific essays, dissertations and specialist books.

Visit us on the internet:

http://www.grin.com/

http://www.facebook.com/grincom

http://www.twitter.com/grin_com

Solving Performance Models based on Basic Queueing Theory Formulas

A study of applicability of Queueing Theory Formulas to Queueing Networks

Bachelor Thesis of

Tatjana Weber

At the Department of Computer Science
Chair for Computer Science II
Software Engineering

Duration: 01. January 2017 — 27. February 2017

Julius-Maximilians-Universität Würzburg

Abstract

The importance and complexity of modern IT systems increased in the last decades. To ensure resource efficiency and Quality-of-Service demands, performance evaluation is useful at every stage in the life cycle of an IT system. Simulation-based performance analysis has a wide application, but computational costs grow the more complex the system of interest gets. However analytical methods have a relatively high accuracy in the performance measures and in efficiency, so results can often be computed significantly faster. This thesis focuses on basic queueing theory. To represent complex IT systems Queueing Network models have been extensively applied. Possibilities and limitations of mapping basic queueing formulas on Queueing Network models are presented by using theoretical knowledge and practical comparison of a self-developed analysis tool with a simulation tool. Deviations in performance measures and savings on computational costs of the analytical solver are shown and by this the usefulness of analytical procedures will be underlined exemplarily.

Zusammenfassung

Die Bedeutung und Komplexität moderner IT-Systeme ist in den letzten Jahrzehnten deutlich angestiegen. Um effiziente Nutzung von Ressourcen und Quality-of-Service Anforderungen zu gewährleisten, ist eine Leistungsbewertung in jedem Lebenszyklus eines IT-Systems nützlich. Simulationsbasierte Werkzeuge zur Leistungsbewertung haben ein breites Anwendungsgebiet, jedoch können die Rechenkosten steigen, je komplexer das zu bewertende System wird. Analytische Methoden sind hingegen sowohl relativ genau wie auch effizient, daher ist ein analytisches Verfahren häufig deutlich schneller. Der Fokus dieser Arbeit liegt auf grundlegenden Erkenntnissen der Warteschlangentheorie. Um komplexe IT-Systeme abzubilden, sind Modelle aus Warteschlangennetzwerken umfassend zum Einsatz gekommen. Möglichkeiten und Grenzen der Anwendung grundlegender Warteschlangenformeln auf Warteschlangennetzwerke werden mit Hilfe von theoretischen Erkenntnissen und praktischen Vergleichen eines selbst entwickelten analytischen Werkzeugs mit einem Simulationswerkzeug präsentiert. Abweichungen der Leistungskennzahlen und Einsparungen an Rechenkosten des analytischen Werkzeugs werden dargestellt und damit der Nutzen analytischer Verfahren exemplarisch unterstrichen.

Contents

1. Introduction

At the beginning of the 21st century computers are omnipresent and widely accepted in both professional and private sectors. The importance and complexity of modern IT systems grew in the last decades. For example, factors such as globalization and outsourcing have led to an increased demand of companies for an effectual IT system and environment. In this context it is significant to ensure resource efficiency and Quality-of-Service demands. A main goal of computer system designers, administrators and users is to obtain or provide a high performance at a low cost. To reach that goal, performance evaluation is useful at every stage in the life cycle of a computer system, e.g. when new systems are designed or existing systems are optimized (reconfiguration, update) or adapted to new environments. The more complex the systems and relations are, the more difficult but also the more important is the analyze. Besides constructing models of IT systems performance prediction analysis is very valuable to finally evaluate these models.

To represent IT systems with a large number of resources, Queueing Network models have been extensively applied. A lot of research has shown that these models are robust and versatile for performance evaluation and prediction. Basic queueing systems were first introduced to study congestion in telephonic system by one service center and then it was extended to analyze congestion in computer and communication systems (cf. [Bal00]). Queueing Network models consist of basic queueing systems. The models are composed of interconnected and interacting service centers/resources and are ideal for mapping modern IT systems. To get performance predictions, several assumptions for Queueing Networks (e.g. for the class of product-form QNs) might be necessary, but they have been recognized to be very powerful models by different researchers.

The analysis of performance models such as Queueing Networks can either be simulation-based or analytical-based. Both approaches share differences, advantages as well as disadvantages. In simulations as well as in analytical processes the input parameters are measured or invented. Simulations are general and have a wide application, while analytical methods, which are based on mathematical relationships, have a set of assumptions and limitations. On the other hand computational costs of simulations grow the more complex the system of interest gets. The big advantage of analytical approaches however is the significantly lower computational costs. E.g. the necessary time to get a result from a simulation is often much longer than by using an analytical formula. Analytical methods have a relatively high accuracy in the performance measures and in efficiency. In cases where computer system designers or administrators want to find the best design or system, they have to compare a number of alternatives, so an analytical tool may be more suitable.

This thesis focuses on an analytical solution of performance metrics. Basic queueing theory formulas are considered because performance results can be computed very fast by them. Possibilities and limitations of mapping the basic formulas on Queueing Network models are presented by using theoretical knowledge and practical comparison of a self-developed analysis tool with an existing simulation tool. Deviations in performance metrics and savings on computational costs of the analytical solver in contrast to a simulation tool are shown and by this the usefulness of analytical procedures will be underlined exemplarily.

The remainder of this paper is divided into six sections. Chapter 2 describes the foundation of this thesis, where queues, Queueing Networks and the solution possibility for system-level performance models are shown. Chapter 3 gives an overview of the main goals and the approach of this paper. In chapter 4 basic queueing formulas are derived and a self-developed tool for solving performance measures of queueing models by analytical formulas is presented. The possibility and the way of mapping basic performance formulas on Queueing Networks is discussed in chapter 5 on a theoretical level. The evaluation of the self-developed solving tool in chapter 6 has a practical aspect. Performance results of the analytical tool and a simulation tool as well as time savings of the analytical procedure are illustrated there. Chapter 7 provides some conclusions and directions for future work.

2. Foundation

This Chapter introduces fundamental concepts and models. Queueing models are described in section 2.1 and afterwards Queueing Networks in section 2.2. Solving system-level performance models is discussed in section 2.3.

2.1 Queues

A queue model is a resource model e.g. of a CPU or disk represented by a waiting line, a service station of one or more servers (single or multiple servers), an arrival and a service process and a scheduling discipline (cf. figure 2.1). The waiting line is a buffer space for waiting elements such as database transactions, batch jobs and different requests called customers. When a server is free, the next customer according to the scheduling discipline will be processed. The scheduling discipline orders which customers are served next at the service station. There are several types, only typical ones will be explained below (cf. [MADD04] and [Kou05]).

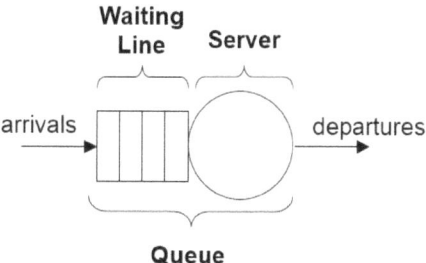

Figure 2.1: single queue with one server

- FCFS/FIFO (First-Come-First-Served / First-In-First-Out): Customers are served in the same order they arrived in.

- LCFS/LIFO (Last-Come-First-Served / Last-In-First-Out): Customers are served in the reverse order they arrived in.

- SIRO (Service-In-Random-Order): Customers are served in a random order independent of the order they arrived in.

- PNPN (Priority Service): Customers with the highest priority are served next. FCFS is used, when the priority is equal. Many variations are possible: static vs. dynamic priorities (priority does not change vs. change with time), preemptive (arrival customer of higher priority directly seize a server which is busy by a lower prioritized customer) vs. non-preemptive.

- RR (Round-Robin): Customers get equal time slices of a defined length and are served according to FCFS.

- PS (Process Sharing): All customers are served simultaneously and the server speed is divided similarly among them. This discipline is like RR but with infinitesimally small time slices.

Moreover, resources/service stations can be grouped in three different types (cf. [MADD04], p. 46):

- Load-independent (LI): Service rate of the resource is constant independent of the load (i.e. number of customers in the queue). Resources such as CPUs and disks are usually load-independent.

- Load-dependant (LD): Service rate is dependant of the load and can be represented by the number of customers in the queue. The service rate can both increase or decrease (depending on the resource) as the number of requests grows.

- Delay (D): Customers are served immediately so there is no waiting line.

Usually Kendall's notation is used to classify a single queueing node by an A/S/m notation which can also be extended to A/S/m/K/N/D (cf. [Kou05]).

- A describes the arrival process (request inter-arrival time distribution).

- S describes the service process (request service time distribution).

- m is the number of servers in the queue.

- K describes the capacity or the maximum number of customers allowed in the queue (incl. those in servers). The number can be limited (finite queue size) but also unlimited (infinite queue size). In the latter case no argument is needed.

- N describes the population size or the maximum allowed number of customers that can arrive in the system. The population size can be limited (finite population size) as well as unlimited (infinite population size). In the latter case no argument is needed.

- D describes the scheduling discipline. For FCFS no argument is needed.

Some possible distributions for the arrival and service processes are:

- M (Markovian) for Poisson or exponential distribution

- D for deterministic (constant) distribution

- E_k for Erlang distribution with scale parameter k

- C_k for Coxian distribution with scale parameter k

- G for general distribution

For example a M/M/1 queue describes a resource with exponentially distributed arrival and service processes. Moreover the queue has a single server, no limitations in capacity and population size and the scheduling discipline is FCFS.

2.2 Queueing Networks

A Queueing Network (QN) is defined as a collection of interconnected queues, which describes an IT system (cf. figure 2.2). Customers move between the queues on a path until they complete their execution. According to their different behaviours, they are often grouped into customer classes, which can either be open or closed.

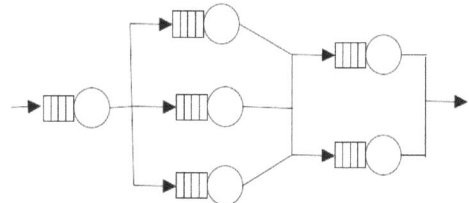

Figure 2.2: Example of a Queueing Network

Customers of an open class arrive from an external source, get served in the QN and depart. The main characteristic is the unbounded population size. The workload is described by an arrival rate. Customers of a closed class do not arrive from an external source and do not depart from the QN but they circulate in the network. Closed classes have a bounded and known number of customers in the system (finite population) and their workload is described by the population size and a think time. In an open QN all customer classes are open, in a closed QN all customer classes are closed and in a mixed QN there are closed and open customer classes.

The network topology describes how the queues are interconnected and how the customers move between them. In figure 2.3 (a) the QN is open and the network topology is tandem, in (b) the QN is closed and the network topology is cyclic. In (c) the QN is also closed and the network topology is central server, where p is the probability that a customer moves to the displayed queue after getting served by the central server queue. The sum of all probabilities have to be one. See [Bal00] for more details.

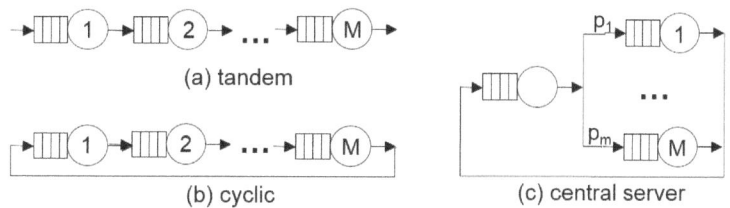

Figure 2.3: Example of queueing network topologies

QNs are often distinguished in product-form and non-product-form, since product-form QNs are easier to analyse. To calculate performance measures of QNs, system steady-state probabilities are to be considered. If the solution of the steady-state probabilities can be expressed as a product of factors describing the state of each queue of a Queueing Network, it is called to be product-form. In other words, product-form Queueing Networks have a simple expression of the stationary state distribution. These QNs have a special structure. Efficient algorithms to evaluate average performance measures were defined for them. The most famous result of product-form QNs is the BCMP theorem (presented by Baskett, Chandy, Muntz and Palacios in 1975). It defined a class of BCMP queueing networks with product-form solutions for open, closed and mixed models with multiple classes of jobs, various service disciplines and service time distributions (cf. [Bal00]). For more information see [Ste09] pp. 598.

2.3 Solving System-Level Performance Models

There are several solution possibilities for performance models depending on the level of performance model and its characterization. This paper focuses on system-level performance models, which have a high abstraction level. In that case the system is viewed as "black-box", where no details are modelled inside the box. A single queue model is of this kind. A model with a lower abstraction level is the component-level model, where different components (e.g. CPUs, disks) and their use by different customers are considered. A Queueing Network model belongs to component-level-models.

2.3.1 Performance Measures and Typical Assumptions

Performance measures or measures of effectiveness are values of certain system properties of e.g. a queueing system. The most commonly obtained measures are explained now (cf. [Ste09]).

The *average system utilization* of a single server is defined as fraction of time that the server is busy and of a multiple server it is defined as the average fraction of servers that are active. The *average system throughput* of customers that are processed per unit time is equal to its departure rate. The *average number of customers* in the system are the customers in the waiting line plus the customers receiving service. At last the *average response time* or *sojourn time* is the time that the request spends in the system from the time it arrived to the queue to the time it departs from the queue. So the response time can be written as the sum of the time the customer spends waiting in the waiting line and the time the customer spends receiving service.

For solving performance models we need some typical assumptions:

- Infinite population assumption: The number of the user population is so large, that the arrival rate does not depend on the number of requests that arrived previously. Hence the arrival process is specified by requests arriving at an average arrival rate of λ requests/sec.

- Homogenous workload assumption: All requests are statistically indistinguishable. Therefore the number of requests present is important and not the individual request.

- Infinite queue assumption: All arriving requests are queued for service, no requests are refused.

- Finite queue assumption: The queue size is limited. In the case that the queue size is fully occupied, arriving requests are refused.

- Operational equilibrium / steady-state assumption: The number of requests present in the system at the start of an observation interval is the same as the number of requests present at the end of the interval. Even though the number of requests in the system may differ between the start and the end of an interval, the error is negligible for reasonably large intervals.

- Markovian / memoryless assumption: The system behaviour is independent of how the system arrived at or how long it has been in a state before. It only depends on the current state. It can be deduced that request inter-arrival times as well as service times are exponentially distributed.

So with these assumptions the focus is on M/M/... queues (cf. Kendall's notation in Chapter 2.2.2), where M stands for Markovian. Markovian queues are the most elementary queueing models.

For dealing with different system-level performance models (cf. chapter 4), results from the generalized system-level model need to be introduced. Specialized models can be derived from the general results by varying different dimensions. These dimensions are the population size (infinite vs. finite population), the service rate (fixed vs. variable service rate) and the queue size (infinite vs. finite queue size).

2.3.2 Generalized System-Level Model

In a generalized system-level model the system can be in different states k. Because of the assumptions above, a state is characterized by the number of requests in the system (requests in waiting line and in service), so $k = 0, 1, \ldots$. Requests arrive at the system (queue) at an arrival rate of λ requests/sec., stand in waiting line for service, get served at a service rate of μ requests/sec. and leave. The arrival rate λ_k and service rate μ_k may be dependent on the state k. Figure 2.4 shows a state transition diagram (STD) for this model.

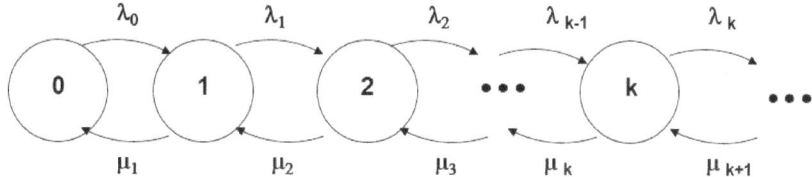

Figure 2.4: State transition diagram - generalized system-level model

Theorem 1. *Let p_k be the probability (or fraction of time), that there are k requests in the system. Then $p_k = p_0 \prod_{i=0}^{k-1} \frac{\lambda_i}{\mu_{i+1}}$ where $p_0 = \left[\sum_{k=0}^{\infty} \prod_{i=0}^{k-1} \frac{\lambda_i}{\mu_{i+1}} \right]^{-1}$*

Proof:

A deduction of the operational equilibrium is that the flow of transitions going into a state k is equal to the flow of transitions going out of the state k for all $k = 0, 1, \ldots$ (flow equilibrium equation / flow-in = flow-out principle). That means

$$\text{flow-in} = \text{flow-out}$$

$$\mu_1 p_1 = \lambda_0 p_0$$

$$\mu_2 p_2 = \lambda_1 p_1$$

$$\ldots$$

$$\mu_k p_k = \lambda_{k-1} p_{k-1}$$

$$\ldots$$

So we can conclude:

$$p_k = \frac{\lambda_{k-1}}{\mu_k} p_{k-1} = \frac{\lambda_{k-1}}{\mu_k} \frac{\lambda_{k-2}}{\mu_{k-1}} p_{k-2} = \cdots = \frac{\lambda_{k-1}}{\mu_k} \frac{\lambda_{k-2}}{\mu_{k-1}} \cdots \frac{\lambda_1}{\mu_2} \frac{\lambda_0}{\mu_1} p_0 = p_0 \prod_{i=0}^{k-1} \frac{\lambda_i}{\mu_{i+1}} \ (*)$$

We also know that the sum of all probabilities is one, so

$$\sum_{k=0}^{\infty} p_k = 1. \text{ With (*) we get } \sum_{k=0}^{\infty} p_0 \prod_{i=0}^{k-1} \frac{\lambda_i}{\mu_{i+1}} = 1 \Leftrightarrow p_0 = \left[\sum_{k=0}^{\infty} \prod_{i=0}^{k-1} \frac{\lambda_i}{\mu_{i+1}} \right]^{-1} \qquad \blacksquare$$

With p_k performance metrics can be defined and computed.

Definition 1. The **system utilization** U is the fraction of time where the system is not idle, so $U = 1 - p_0$.

Note that the definition of the utilization for multiple server queues differ from the definition of [Ste09], which was presented in section 2.3.1.

Definition 2. The **system throughput** X is the rate, at which requests are completed from a system so $X = \sum\limits_{k=1}^{\infty} \mu_k p_k$.

Definition 3. The **average number of requests** N can be written as $N = \sum\limits_{k=1}^{\infty} k \times p_k$.

Theorem 1. The **average response time** R can be expressed by $R = \frac{N}{X}$.

Proof:

For this equation we use Little's Law, which says that the average number of customers in a system in long-term is equal to the average throughput of that system multiplied by the average time requests stay in the system (for further information see [MA98] pp. 65-67).

$N = X \times R \Leftrightarrow R = \frac{N}{X}$ ∎

Note: All equations are from [MA98].

3. Goals and Approach

This chapter describes goals of this bachelor thesis, gives an overview of the approach and of some restrictions. In section 3.1 the main goal and subgoals are defined. A theoretical and practical procedure for each subgoal is summarized, too. The approach is explained more detailed in section 3.2.

3.1 Goals

The main goal of this thesis is the analytical solving of product-form Queueing Network models based on basic Queueing Theory Formulas. The solving methods are aimed at performance metrics like user count, utilization, throughput and response time. The main goal can be divided into the following subgoals.

G1: Choose queueing models and automate the calculation of the average number of customers, the throughput, the utilization and the response time of them.

- theoretical part: derive all four performance formulas for the specialized system-level models from the generalized system-level model.

- practical part: implement an analytical performance analyzing tool based on the derived formulas - the Markovian Queue Solver.

G2: Apply the basic queueing formulas on selected Queueing Network models.

- theoretical part: determine possibilities and limitations/restrictions of mapping basic queueing formulas on open and closed Queueing Network models.

- practical part: evaluate theoretical results by comparing performance results and time savings of the self-developed analytical tool (applied on QNs) with a simulation tool.

3.2 Approach

An theoretical and practical approach of both subgoals was briefly mentioned in the section before and is now clarified more precisely.

Theoretical part of the approach for G1: *derive all four performance formulas of the specialized system-level models from the generalized system-level model.*

Different specialized system-level models (queues) with specific formulas and input parameters can be derived from the generalized system-level model by varying three characteristics: workload type, number of servers and capacity. Each of them are markovian queues with exponentially distributed arrival and service rates. Since only product-form Queueing Networks are considered, the scheduling discipline of the queues is restricted to FCFS, LCFS, PS and IS (only that type of queues possess local balance and fulfil the BCMP theorem, cf. [Ste09] pp. 598). Solution formulas of the specified queues are independent of the four mentioned scheduling disciplines, because they have just an effect on the distribution of the performance measures and not on the average results. In the following the specified system-level models are described by Kendall's notation (cf. chapter 2.2). The only difference to the regulare use of Kendall's notation is that if no scheduling discipline is set, then the queue can have FCFS, LCFS, PS or IS discipline (not only FCFS).

The table below offers an overview of possible system-level models.

queue	workload		server			capacity	
characteritics	open	closed	single	multiple	delay	infinite	finite
M/M/1	x		x			x	
M/M/m	x			x		x	
M/M/1/K	x		x				x
M/M/m/K	x			x			x
M/M/1/∞/N		x	x			x	
M/M/m/∞/N		x		x		x	
M/M/1/K/N		x	x				x
M/M/m/K/N		x		x			x
M/M/∞	x				x	-	-
M/M/ ∞ / ∞ /K		x			x	-	-

Queues with open and closed workload, with single and multiple servers and with finite and infinite capacity are considered in this thesis while delay resources are not in focus. The specified queueing formulas are derived analytically from the generalized system-level model.

Practical part of the approach for G1: *implement an analytical performance analyzing tool based on the derived formulas - the Markovian Queue Solver.*

In order to analyse the application of the formulas to Queueing Networks, we automated the calculations of performance metrics of queues by developing a solution tool called the Markovian Queue Solver. Time savings and reduced errors are the advantages of such a tool (as opposed to manual calculations). We also compared performance results of the analytical solver with results of a simulation.

There are two possibilities referring to the Markovian Queue Solver. Either a new solution-tool could be implemented or an existing excel document (from [MA98]) could be customized. Disadvantages by using the excel document are, that the formulas, which are implemented in VBA (Visual Basic for Applications is an application edition of Microsoft's Visual Basic programming language), are not explicitly designed for solving models with more servers (there are only formulas available for queues with variable service rates, where a saturation point is necessary). Furthermore the VBA programming was done with an older excel-version, so there are some problems if this excel document is used with a current excel version. An advantage would be that some of the relevant formulas are implemented already. Advantages of a newly implemented tool are better manageability for test since we could run several tests over a loop. In addition, the tool could be more easily integrated into other projects. Therefore, the decision was made to develop a new tool. That tool was implemented with Java in an eclipse environment.

Theoretical part of the approach for G2: *determine possibilities and limitations/ restrictions of mapping basic queueing formulas on open and closed Queueing Network models.*

The next step was to apply the implemented basic queueing formulas to Queueing Networks. The analyzed QNs consist of the markovian queues mentioned above and can either be open or closed with one or more customer classes. They meet the BCMP theorem and are product-form (cf. [Ste09] pp. 598). First, open QNs with tandem topology and routing probabilities are considered and then closed QNs are discussed.

The workload of QNs is described for the complete system but not for each individual queue. Since the basic queueing formulas are just for queues and not for a QN, the big challenge is to determine the interarrival rates for the corresponding queues. The interarrival rate of a queue is equal to the throughput (or departure rate) of the previous queue in a steady-state equilibrium. The idea is that if the throughput can be determined, the basic formulas can be used. Possible solutions will be discussed at a conceptual level.

Practical part of the approach for G2: *evaluate theoretical results by comparing performance results and time savings of the self-developed analytical tool (applied on QNs) with a simulation tool.*

An evaluation fo the Markovian Queue Solver is the last step of this paper, which is carried out by comparison with a simulation tool. For the simulation JSIMgraph is used, which is part of Java Modeling Tools (JMT). JMT is a tool for simulating and analysing QNs. It offers six applications: JSIMwiz, JSIMgraph, JMVA, JABA, JWAT, and JMCH. JSIMwiz and JSIMgraph are very similar, JSIMgraph offers the same functionality but provides a model simulator with graphical user interface while JSIMwiz provides a model simulator with wizard-based user interface. They support open, closed and mixed QNs. Several routing strategies, time distributions (for arrival and service rates) and scheduling disciplines are available as well as different numbers of servers, capacity limitations and a lot of other features. A transformation from JSIM to JMVA for product-form Queueing Networks is also possible at JMT. JMVA offers analytical solutions by using the Mean Value Analysis (MVA) algorithm of open, closed and mixed QNs, so results from there can optionally be included for comparisons. Further information about JMT can be found in [JMT]. Some parameters we used to create Queueing Network models in JSIMGraph are summarized next.

Modelsthat we looked at were designed with exponentially distributed arrival and service rates. The routing strategy for QNs with tandem topology was set to random and for QNs with routing probabilities to probability. PS without priority was used as scheduling policy. Furthermore the confidence interval was set to 0.99 and the maximum relative error to 0.03.

4. Markovian Queue Solver

This chapter includes the different types of resources and their performance formulas and finally presents the implemented *Markovian Queue Solver*. In section 4.1 performance-relevant parameters are defined and explained. Thereafter, formulas for eight different specialized system-level models are derived from the generalized system-level model. Section 4.2 gives an overview of the performance solution tool, which is implemented in Java and based on the queueing formulas.

4.1 Performance Formulas of Markovian Queues

In this section performance formulas of eight specialized system-level models (queues) are presented. They vary in workload type (open vs. closed), in number of servers (single vs. multiple) and in capacity (finite vs. infinite) and are all derived from the generalized system-level model. Used equations of the generalized model are (cf. section 2.3.2 or [MA98]):

$$p_k = p_0 \prod_{i=0}^{k-1} \frac{\lambda_i}{\mu_{i+1}} \text{ where } p_0 = \left[\sum_{k=0}^{\infty} \prod_{i=0}^{k-1} \frac{\lambda_i}{\mu_{i+1}} \right]^{-1} \tag{4.1}$$

$$U = 1 - p_0 \tag{4.2}$$

$$X = \sum_{k=1}^{\infty} \mu_k p_k \tag{4.3}$$

$$N = \sum_{k=1}^{\infty} k \times p_k \tag{4.4}$$

They consist of variable arrival and service rates, which are not further described. For specialized models the mentioned rates can be precisely defined and used in the generalized formulas. Furthermore the generalized model consists of equations which sum up to infinity. So for queues with open workload and infinite capacity, formulas of infinite geometric series can be used (with some restrictions) to derive a finite sum. For all other queues with closed workload or capacity limitations, a finite sum can be derived from the generalized model since the number of possible states is finite. For further simplification formulas of finite geometric series can be included.

First some necessary symbols and parameters are defined in addition to the used ones of the generalized system-level model:

- K describes the capacity like it is used in Kendall's Notation. Note that K can never be less than the number of servers in a queue.

- M is the maximum allowed number of requests, that can arrive in the system (N in Kendall's Notation), if population is finite.

- z is the think time rate in requests/sec. and is also part of a finite population. The think time Z is the time spent by the client from the time a response to a transaction is received and the next transaction is submitted ([MADD04], p. 191), so $z = \frac{1}{Z}$.

- m describes the number of servers in a queue like it is used in Kendall's Notation.

Next we shall consider the service and arrival rates that are variable in the generalized system-level model. Depending on the characteristics of the analysed queues, they can either be fix or variable.

Arrival rates are defined by the workload. An open workload is described by a fixed arrival rate. However a closed workload has M variable arrival rates as shown in the state transition diagram (with $M + 1$ states).

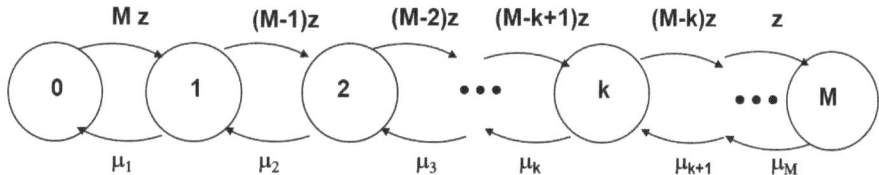

Figure 4.1: State transition diagram of a finite population

Each of the M clients can either be in the think time (their job is not in the system), or waiting to receive a submitted transaction (their job is in the system). In state k, k transactions submitted by k of the M clients are in the system. Therefore there are $M - k$ clients in the think time, who submit their transactions each with the think time rate z. So $\lambda_k = (M - k)z$ for all possible states $0 \leq k < M$ (see [MA98] for more information). Similar finite capacity K can be included in the definition of the arrival rates for open and closed models. For all states $0 \leq k < K$ (open model) or $0 \leq k < min\{M, K\}$ (closed model) they are as described above and otherwise they are zero. Arrival rates are explicitly defined in the corresponding subsections.

Now the service rates should be considered. In a single server model service rates are fixed, while in a multiple server model service rates of the system depend on the system state (load dependent). Let μ be the service rate of each server. If the number of requests k is smaller or equal to the number of servers, k servers are busy and each one services a request by a rate of μ, so the service rate of the system in state k is $\lambda_k = k\mu$. The service rate of the system saturates by $\lambda_k = m\mu$, if there are equal or more requests than the number of the servers m. The following diagram illustrates this context (see [MA98] for more information). The explicit definition of the service rates can be found in the following subsections.

In order to solve the performance metrics, the corresponding arrival and service rates are chosen and used in the formulas of the generalized system-level model. By using them

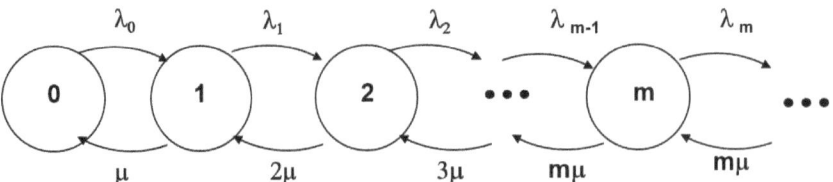

Figure 4.2: State transition diagram of a multiple server model

and by applying equations of geometric series, performance formulas can be determined for the individual queues.

Used formulas of infinite geometric series if $|q| < 1$:

$$\sum_{k=0}^{\infty} q^k = \frac{1}{1-q} \tag{4.5}$$

$$\sum_{k=0}^{\infty} kq^k = \frac{q}{(1-q)^2} \tag{4.6}$$

Used (generalized) formulas of finite geometric series if $q \neq 1$:

$$\sum_{k=a}^{b} q^k = \frac{q^a - q^{b+1}}{1-q} \tag{4.7}$$

$$\sum_{k=0}^{b} kq^k = \frac{bq^{b+2} - (b+1)q^{b+1} + q}{(1-q)^2} \tag{4.8}$$

$$\sum_{k=0}^{n} k = \frac{n(n+1)}{2} \tag{4.9}$$

The average system utilization U, average system throughput X and average number of requests N are derived for the individual queues. The average response time R is $R = \frac{N}{X}$ (see section 2.3.2) for all queues and it is therefore not explicitly considered in the subsections.

4.1.1 M/M/1 Queue

Arrival and service rates can be represented by $\lambda_k = \lambda$ for all $k \geq 0$ and $\mu_k = \mu$ for all $k > 0$. Let further be $\frac{\lambda}{\mu} < 1$ (necessary condition for the application of the infinite geometric series, otherwise it is not solvable). Following results can be derived from the generalized system-level model:

$$p_0 \overset{(1)}{=} \left[\sum_{k=0}^{\infty} \prod_{i=0}^{k-1} \frac{\lambda_i}{\mu_{i+1}}\right]^{-1} \overset{(2)}{=} \left[\sum_{k=0}^{\infty} (\frac{\lambda}{\mu})^k\right]^{-1} \overset{(3)}{=} \left[\frac{1}{1-\frac{\lambda}{\mu}}\right]^{-1} = 1 - \frac{\lambda}{\mu} \tag{4.10}$$

Note: (1) cf. equation (4.1); (2) use defined λ_k and μ_k; (3) use geometric series (cf. equation (4.5))

$$p_k \overset{(1)}{=} p_0 \prod_{i=0}^{k-1} \frac{\lambda_i}{\mu_{i+1}} \overset{(2)}{=} p_0 (\frac{\lambda}{\mu})^k \tag{4.11}$$

Note: (1) cf. equation (4.1); (2) use defined λ_k and μ_k

$$U \overset{(1)}{=} 1 - p_0 \overset{(2)}{=} 1 - (1 - \frac{\lambda}{\mu}) = \frac{\lambda}{\mu} \tag{4.12}$$

Note: (1) cf. equation (4.2); (2) cf. equation 4.10

$$X \overset{(1)}{=} \sum_{k=1}^{\infty} \mu_k p_k \overset{(2)}{=} \mu \sum_{k=1}^{\infty} p_k \overset{(3)}{=} \mu(1 - p_0) \overset{(4)}{=} \mu \frac{\lambda}{\mu} = \lambda \tag{4.13}$$

Note: (1) cf. equation (4.3); (2) use defined μ_k; (3) sum of all probabilities is one; (4) cf. equation (4.10)

$$N \overset{(1)}{=} \sum_{k=1}^{\infty} k \times p_k \overset{(2)}{=} \sum_{k=1}^{\infty} k \times p_0 (\frac{\lambda}{\mu})^k + 0 \times p_0 \overset{(3)}{=} p_0 \sum_{k=0}^{\infty} k \times (\frac{\lambda}{\mu})^k \overset{(4)}{=} p_0 \frac{\frac{\lambda}{\mu}}{(1 - \frac{\lambda}{\mu})^2}$$

$$\overset{(5)}{=} (1 - \frac{\lambda}{\mu}) \frac{\frac{\lambda}{\mu}}{(1 - \frac{\lambda}{\mu})^2} \overset{(6)}{=} \frac{\lambda}{\mu - \lambda} \tag{4.14}$$

Note: (1) cf. equation (4.4); (2) use defined λ_k and add zero; (4) form infinite geometric series; (5) use geometric series (cf. equation (4.6))

Attention: Performance metrics of M/M/1 queues are not solvable if $\lambda \geq \mu$!

4.1.2 M/M/m Queue

Arrival and service rates can be represented by $\lambda_k = \lambda$ for all $k \geq 0$ and

$$\mu_k = \begin{cases} k\mu & \text{for } 0 < k \leq m \\ m\mu & \text{for } k \geq m \end{cases}$$

Furthermore let ρ be $\rho = \frac{\lambda}{m\mu} < 1$ (necessary condition for the application of the infinite geometric series, otherwise it is not solvable). Following results can be derived from the generalized system-level model:

$$p_0 \overset{(1)}{=} \left[\sum_{k=0}^{\infty} \prod_{i=0}^{k-1} \frac{\lambda_i}{\mu_{i+1}} \right]^{-1} \overset{(2)}{=} \left[1 + \sum_{k=1}^{m-1} \frac{\lambda^k}{\mu^k k!} + \sum_{k=m}^{\infty} \frac{\lambda^k}{m! m^{k-m} \mu^k} \right]^{-1} \overset{(3)}{=} \left[1 + \sum_{k=1}^{m-1} \frac{\lambda^k}{\mu^k k!} + \frac{m^m}{m!} \sum_{k=m}^{\infty} \rho^k \right]^{-1}$$

$$\overset{(4)}{=} \left[1 + \sum_{k=1}^{m-1} \frac{\lambda^k}{\mu^k k!} + \frac{m^m}{m!} \left(\sum_{k=0}^{\infty} \rho^k - \sum_{k=0}^{m-1} \rho^k \right) \right]^{-1} \overset{(5)}{=} \left[1 + \sum_{k=1}^{m-1} \frac{\lambda^k}{\mu^k k!} + \frac{m^m}{m!} \left(\frac{1}{1-\rho} - \frac{1-\rho^m}{1-\rho} \right) \right]^{-1}$$

$$= \left[1 + \sum_{k=1}^{m-1} \frac{\lambda^k}{\mu^k k!} + \frac{(m\rho)^m}{m!} \frac{1}{1-\rho} \right]^{-1} \tag{4.15}$$

Note: (1) cf. equation (4.1); (2) partial sum and use defined λ_k and μ_k; (3) change mathematical expression and use ρ; (4) form infinite geometric series; (5) use geometric series (cf. equation (4.5) and (4.7))

$$p_k \overset{(1)}{=} p_0 \prod_{i=0}^{k-1} \frac{\lambda_i}{\mu_{i+1}} \overset{(2)}{=} \begin{cases} p_0 \frac{\lambda^k}{\mu^k k!} & \text{for } 0 < k \leq m \\ p_0 \frac{m^m}{m!} \rho^k & \text{for } k \geq m \\ 0 & \text{else} \end{cases} \tag{4.16}$$

Note: (1) cf. equation (4.1); (2) use defined λ_k, μ_k and ρ

$$U = 1 - p_0 \text{ (cf. equation (4.2))} \tag{4.17}$$

$X = \lambda$ (since it is an open model with unbounded queue size [MA98] p. 189) $\qquad$ (4.18)

$$N \overset{(1)}{=} \sum_{k=1}^{\infty} k \times p_k \overset{(2)}{=} \sum_{k=1}^{m} k \times p_k + p_0 \frac{m^m}{m!} \sum_{k=m+1}^{\infty} k \times \rho^k \overset{(3)}{=} \sum_{k=1}^{m} k \times p_k + p_0 \frac{m^m}{m!} \left(\sum_{k=0}^{\infty} k \times \rho^k - \sum_{k=0}^{m} k \times \rho^k \right)$$

$$\overset{(4)}{=} \sum_{k=1}^{m} k \times p_k + p_0 \frac{m^m}{m!} \left(\frac{\rho}{(1-\rho)^2} - \frac{m\rho^{m+2} - (m+1)\rho^{m+1} + \rho}{(1-\rho)^2} \right)$$

$$= \sum_{k=1}^{m} k \times p_k + p_0 \frac{m^m}{m!} \frac{\rho^{m+1}(1 + m - m\rho)}{(1-\rho)^2} \qquad (4.19)$$

Note: (1) cf. equation (4.4); (2) partial sum and use equation (4.16); (3) form infinite geometric series; (4) use geometric series (cf. equation (4.6) and (4.8))

Attention: Performance metrics of M/M/m queues are not solvable if $\lambda \geq m\mu$!

4.1.3 M/M/1/∞/N Queue

Arrival and service rates can be represented by $\mu_k = \mu$ for all $k > 0$ and

$$\lambda_k = \begin{cases} (M - k)z & \text{for } 0 \leq k < M \\ 0 & \text{else} \end{cases}$$

Following results can be derived from the generalized system-level model:

$$p_0 \overset{(1)}{=} \left[\sum_{k=0}^{\infty} \prod_{i=0}^{k-1} \frac{\lambda_i}{\mu_{i+1}} \right]^{-1} \overset{(2)}{=} \left[\sum_{k=0}^{M} \prod_{i=0}^{k-1} \frac{z(M-k)}{\mu} \right]^{-1} \overset{(3)}{=} \left[M! \sum_{k=0}^{M} \frac{z^k}{(M-k)!\mu^k} \right]^{-1} \qquad (4.20)$$

Note: (1) cf. equation (4.1); (2) use defined λ_k and μ_k; (3) it applies $\prod_{i=0}^{k-1} M - k = \frac{M!}{(M-k)!}$

$$p_k \overset{(1)}{=} p_0 \prod_{i=0}^{k-1} \frac{\lambda_i}{\mu_{i+1}} \overset{(2)}{=} \begin{cases} p_0 \prod_{i=0}^{k-1} \frac{z(M-k)}{\mu} \overset{(3)}{=} p_0 \frac{M!z^k}{(M-k)!\mu^k} & \text{for } 0 < k \leq M \\ 0 & \text{else} \end{cases} \qquad (4.21)$$

Note: (1) cf. equation (4.1); (2) use defined λ_k and μ_k; (3) it applies $\prod_{i=0}^{k-1} M - k = \frac{M!}{(M-k)!}$

$U = 1 - p_0$ (cf. equation (4.2)) $\qquad$ (4.22)

$$X \overset{(1)}{=} \sum_{k=1}^{\infty} \mu_k p_k \overset{(2)}{=} \mu \sum_{k=1}^{\infty} p_k \overset{(3)}{=} \mu(1 - p_0) \overset{(4)}{=} \mu \times U \qquad (4.23)$$

Note: (1) cf. equation (4.3); (2) use defined μ_k; (3) sum of all probabilities is one; (4) cf. equation (4.22)

$$N \overset{(1)}{=} \sum_{k=1}^{\infty} k \times p_k \overset{(2)}{=} \sum_{k=1}^{M} k \times p_k \qquad (4.24)$$

Note: (1) cf. equation (4.4); (2) cf. equation (4.21)

4.1.4 M/M/m/∞/N Queue

Arrival and service rates can be represented by

$$\lambda_k = \begin{cases} (M-k)z & \text{for } 0 \le k < M \\ 0 & \text{else} \end{cases}$$

$$\mu_k = \begin{cases} k\mu & \text{for } 0 < k \le m \\ m\mu & \text{for } k \ge m \end{cases}$$

Furthermore let ρ be $\rho = \frac{z}{m\mu}$. Following results can be derived from the generalized system-level model:

$$p_0 \stackrel{(1)}{=} \left[\sum_{k=0}^{\infty} \prod_{i=0}^{k-1} \frac{\lambda_i}{\mu_{i+1}} \right]^{-1} \stackrel{(2)}{=} \left[1 + \sum_{k=1}^{min\{m,M\}} \prod_{i=0}^{k-1} \frac{z(M-k)}{k\mu} + \sum_{k=m+1}^{M} \prod_{i=0}^{k-1} \frac{z(M-k)}{\mu_{i+1}} + 0 \right]^{-1}$$

$$\stackrel{(3)}{=} \left[1 + \sum_{k=1}^{min\{m,M\}} \frac{M!z^k}{(M-k)!k!\mu^k} + \sum_{k=m+1}^{M} \frac{M!z^k}{(M-k)!m!m^{k-m}\mu^k} \right]^{-1}$$

$$= \left[1 + M! \left(\sum_{k=1}^{min\{m,M\}} \frac{z^k}{(M-k)!k!\mu^k} + \frac{m^m}{m!} \sum_{k=m+1}^{M} \frac{1}{(M-k)!}\rho^k \right) \right]^{-1} \tag{4.25}$$

Note: (1) cf. equation (4.1); (2) partial sum and use defined λ_k and μ_k; (3) since it applies

$$\prod_{i=0}^{k-1} M-k = \frac{M!}{(M-k)!} \text{ and } \prod_{i=0}^{k-1} \frac{1}{\mu_{i+1}} = \frac{1}{m!m^{k-m}} \text{ for } k > m$$

$$p_k \stackrel{(1)}{=} p_0 \prod_{i=0}^{k-1} \frac{\lambda_i}{\mu_{i+1}} \stackrel{(2)}{=} \begin{cases} p_0 \prod_{i=0}^{k-1} \frac{z(M-k)}{k\mu} \stackrel{(3)}{=} p_0 \frac{M!z^k}{(M-k)!k!\mu^k} & \text{for } 0 < k \le min\{m,M\} \\ p_0 \prod_{i=0}^{k-1} \frac{z(M-k)}{\mu_{i+1}} \stackrel{(3)}{=} p_0 \frac{M!m^m}{(M-k)!m!}\rho^k & \text{for } m < k \le M \\ 0 & \text{else} \end{cases} \tag{4.26}$$

Note: (1) cf. equation (4.1); (2) use defined λ_k and μ_k; (3) since it applies

$$\prod_{i=0}^{k-1} M-k = \frac{M!}{(M-k)!} \text{ and } \prod_{i=0}^{k-1} \frac{1}{\mu_{i+1}} = \frac{1}{m!m^{k-m}} \text{ for } k > m$$

$$U = 1 - p_0 \text{ (cf. equation (4.2))} \tag{4.27}$$

$$X \stackrel{(1)}{=} \sum_{k=1}^{\infty} \mu_k p_k \stackrel{(2)}{=} \sum_{k=1}^{min\{m,M\}} k\mu p_k + \sum_{k=m+1}^{M} m\mu p_k = \mu \left(\sum_{k=1}^{min\{m,M\}} k p_k + m \sum_{k=m+1}^{M} p_k \right) \tag{4.28}$$

Note: (1) cf. equation (4.3); (2) use defined μ_k and equation (4.26)

$$N \stackrel{(1)}{=} \sum_{k=1}^{\infty} k \times p_k \stackrel{(2)}{=} \sum_{k=1}^{M} k \times p_k \tag{4.29}$$

Note: (1) cf. equation (4.4); (2) cf. equation (4.26)

Attention: The specific case $m < M$ for M/M/m/∞/N queue can also be seen as a delay resource type.

4.1.5 M/M/1/K Queue

Arrival and service rates can be represented by $\mu_k = \mu$ for all $k > 0$ and

$$\lambda_k = \begin{cases} \lambda & \text{for } 0 \leq k < K \\ 0 & \text{else} \end{cases}$$

Furthermore let ρ be $\rho = \frac{\lambda}{\mu} \neq 1$. Following results can be derived from the generalized system-level model:

$$p_0 \overset{(1)}{=} \left[\sum_{k=0}^{\infty} \prod_{i=0}^{k-1} \frac{\lambda_i}{\mu_{i+1}} \right]^{-1} \overset{(2)}{=} \left[\sum_{k=0}^{K} \frac{\lambda}{\mu} \right]^{-1} \overset{(3)}{=} \left[\frac{1 - \rho^{K+1}}{1 - \rho} \right]^{-1} = \frac{1 - \rho}{1 - \rho^{K+1}} \tag{4.30}$$

Note: (1) cf. equation (4.1); (2) use defined λ_k and μ_k; (3) use geometric series (cf. equation (4.9)

$$p_k \overset{(1)}{=} p_0 \prod_{i=0}^{k-1} \frac{\lambda_i}{\mu_{i+1}} \overset{(2)}{=} \begin{cases} p_0 \times \rho^k & \text{for } 0 < k \leq K \\ 0 & \text{else} \end{cases} \tag{4.31}$$

Note: (1) cf. equation (4.1); (2) use defined λ_k and μ_k;

$$U = 1 - p_0 \quad (\text{cf. equation } (4.2)) \tag{4.32}$$

$$X \overset{(1)}{=} \sum_{k=1}^{\infty} \mu_k p_k \overset{(2)}{=} \mu \sum_{k=1}^{K} p_k \overset{(3)}{=} \mu(1 - p_0) \overset{(4)}{=} \mu \times U \tag{4.33}$$

Note: (1) cf. equation (4.3); (2) use defined μ_k and equation (4.31) (3) sum of all probabilities p_k, $k = 0, 1, ..., K$ is one; (4) cf. equation (4.32)

$$N \overset{(1)}{=} \sum_{k=1}^{\infty} k \times p_k \overset{(2)}{=} p_0 \sum_{k=1}^{K} k \times \rho^k \overset{(3)}{=} p_0 \sum_{k=0}^{K} k \times \rho^k \overset{(4)}{=} p_0 \frac{K\rho^{K+2} - (K+1)\rho^{K+1} + \rho}{(1 - \rho)^2} \tag{4.34}$$

Note: (1) cf. equation (4.4); (2) cf. equation (4.31) (3) add zero to form finite geometric series (4) use geometric series (cf. equation (4.8)

For the specific case that $\rho = \frac{\lambda}{\mu} = 1$, following equations can be derived.

$$p_0 \overset{(1)}{=} \left[\sum_{k=0}^{\infty} \prod_{i=0}^{k-1} \frac{\lambda_i}{\mu_{i+1}} \right]^{-1} \overset{(2)}{=} \left[\sum_{k=0}^{K} \frac{\lambda}{\mu} \right]^{-1} \overset{(3)}{=} \left[\sum_{k=0}^{K} 1 \right]^{-1} = \frac{1}{K+1} \tag{4.35}$$

Note: (1) cf. equation (4.1); (2) use defined λ_k and μ_k; (3) use defined ρ

$$p_k \overset{(1)}{=} p_0 \prod_{i=0}^{k-1} \frac{\lambda_i}{\mu_{i+1}} \overset{(2)}{=} \begin{cases} p_0 & \text{for } 0 < k \leq K \\ 0 & \text{else} \end{cases} \tag{4.36}$$

Note: (1) cf. equation (4.1); (2) use defined λ_k, μ_k and ρ

$$N \overset{(1)}{=} \sum_{k=1}^{\infty} k \times p_k \overset{(2)}{=} p_0 \sum_{k=1}^{K} k \overset{(3)}{=} p_0 \frac{K(K+1)}{2} \tag{4.37}$$

Note: (1) cf. equation (4.4); (2) cf. equation (4.36) (3) use geometric series (cf. equation (4.9)

The equations for the average throughput X and the average utilization U remain unchanged, only the stated probabilities are to be used for the calculation.

4.1.6 M/M/m/K Queue

Arrival and service rates can be represented by

$$\lambda_k = \begin{cases} \lambda & \text{for } 0 \le k < K \\ 0 & \text{else} \end{cases}$$

$$\mu_k = \begin{cases} k\mu & \text{for } 0 < k \le m \\ m\mu & \text{for } k \ge m \end{cases}$$

Furthermore let ρ be $\rho = \frac{\lambda}{m\mu} \ne 1$. Following results can be derived from the generalized system-level model:

$$p_0 \overset{(1)}{=} \left[\sum_{k=0}^{\infty} \prod_{i=0}^{k-1} \frac{\lambda_i}{\mu_{i+1}} \right]^{-1} \overset{(2)}{=} \left[1 + \sum_{k=1}^{m} \prod_{i=0}^{k-1} \frac{\lambda}{k\mu} + \sum_{k=m+1}^{K} \prod_{i=0}^{k-1} \frac{\lambda}{\mu_{i+1}} + 0 \right]^{-1}$$

$$\overset{(3)}{=} \left[1 + \sum_{k=1}^{m} \frac{\lambda^k}{k!\mu^k} + \sum_{k=m+1}^{K} \frac{\lambda^k}{m!m^{k-m}\mu^k} \right]^{-1} \overset{(4)}{=} \left[1 + \sum_{k=1}^{m} \frac{\lambda^k}{k!\mu^k} + \frac{m^m}{m!} \sum_{k=m+1}^{K} \rho^k \right]^{-1}$$

$$\overset{(5)}{=} \left[1 + \sum_{k=1}^{m} \frac{\lambda^k}{k!\mu^k} + \frac{m^m}{m!} \frac{\rho^{m+1} - \rho^{K+1}}{1 - \rho} \right]^{-1} \left[1 + \sum_{k=1}^{m} \frac{\lambda^k}{k!\mu^k} + \frac{\rho(m\rho)^m(1 - \rho^{K-m})}{m!(1 - \rho)} \right]^{-1} \quad (4.38)$$

Note: (1) cf. equation (4.1); (2) partial sum and use defined λ_k and μ_k; (3) since it applies and $\prod_{i=0}^{k-1} \frac{1}{\mu_{i+1}} = \frac{1}{m!m^{k-m}}$ for $k > m$ (4) use defined ρ (5) use geometric series (cf. equation (4.7))

$$p_k \overset{(1)}{=} p_0 \prod_{i=0}^{k-1} \frac{\lambda_i}{\mu_{i+1}} \overset{(2)}{=} \begin{cases} p_0 \frac{\lambda^k}{k!\mu^k} & \text{for } 0 < k \le m \\ p_0 \frac{m^m}{m!} \rho^k & \text{for } m < k \le K \\ 0 & \text{else} \end{cases} \quad (4.39)$$

Note: (1) cf. equation (4.1); (2) use defined λ_k, μ_k, the equation $\prod_{i=0}^{k-1} \frac{1}{\mu_{i+1}} = \frac{1}{m!m^{k-m}}$ for $k > m$ and ρ

$$U = 1 - p_0 \quad \text{(cf. equation (4.2))} \quad (4.40)$$

$$X \overset{(1)}{=} \sum_{k=1}^{\infty} \mu_k p_k \overset{(2)}{=} \sum_{k=1}^{m} k\mu p_k + \sum_{k=m+1}^{K} m\mu p_k = \mu \left(\sum_{k=1}^{m} k p_k + m \sum_{k=m+1}^{K} p_k \right) \quad (4.41)$$

Note: (1) cf. equation (4.3); (2) partial sum and use defined μ_k and equation (4.39) where $p_k = 0$ for $k > K$

$$N \overset{(1)}{=} \sum_{k=1}^{\infty} k \times p_k \overset{(2)}{=} \sum_{k=1}^{K} k \times p_k \quad (4.42)$$

Note: (1) cf. equation (4.4); (2) cf. equation (4.39) where $p_k = 0$ for $k > K$

For the specific case that $\rho = \frac{\lambda}{m\mu} = 1$, following equations can be derived.

$$p_0 \overset{(1)}{=} \left[1 + \sum_{k=1}^{m} \frac{\lambda^k}{k!\mu^k} + \frac{m^m}{m!} \sum_{k=m+1}^{K} \rho^k \right]^{-1} \overset{(2)}{=} \left[1 + \sum_{k=1}^{m} \frac{\lambda^k}{k!\mu^k} + \frac{m^m(K-m)}{m!} \right]^{-1} \tag{4.43}$$

Note: (1) cf. steps in equation (4.38) (2) use $\rho = 1$

$$p_k \overset{(1)}{=} p_0 \prod_{i=0}^{k-1} \frac{\lambda_i}{\mu_{i+1}} \overset{(2)}{=} \begin{cases} p_0 \frac{\lambda^k}{k!\mu^k} & \text{for } 0 < k \leq m \\ p_0 \frac{m^m}{m!} & \text{for } m < k \leq K \\ 0 & \text{else} \end{cases} \tag{4.44}$$

Note: (1) cf. equation (4.1); (2) use defined λ_k, μ_k and ρ

The equations for the average throughput X, the average utilization U and the average number of requests N remain unchanged, only the stated probabilities are to be used for the calculation.

Attention: By definition of capacity applies $K \geq m!$ Capacity is the maximum allowed number of customers in the waiting line plus in service (at least m customers can be in a queue).

4.1.7 M/M/1/K/N Queue

Arrival and service rates can be represented by $\mu_k = \mu$ for $0 < k$ and

$$\lambda_k = \begin{cases} (M-k)z & \text{for } 0 \leq k < min\{M, K\} \\ 0 & \text{else} \end{cases}$$

Following results can be derived from the generalized system-level model, analogue to the M/M/1/∞/N Queue.

$$p_0 = \left[M! \sum_{k=0}^{min\{M,K\}} \frac{z^k}{(M-k)!\mu^k} \right]^{-1} \tag{4.45}$$

$$p_k = \begin{cases} p_0 \frac{M!z^k}{(M-k)!\mu^k} & \text{for } 0 < k \leq min\{M, K\} \\ 0 & \text{else} \end{cases} \tag{4.46}$$

$$U = 1 - p_0 \tag{4.47}$$

$$X = \mu \times U \tag{4.48}$$

$$N = \sum_{k=1}^{min\{M,K\}} k \times p_k \tag{4.49}$$

Attention: If $M \leq K$ the performance formulas of M/M/1/K/N queue are equal to the formulas of a M/M/1/∞/N queue.

4.1.8 M/M/m/K/N Queue

Arrival and service rates can be represented by

$$\lambda_k = \begin{cases} (M-k)z & \text{for } 0 \leq k < min\{M,K\} \\ 0 & \text{else} \end{cases}$$

$$\mu_k = \begin{cases} k\mu & \text{for } 0 < k \leq m \\ m\mu & \text{for } k \geq m \end{cases}$$

Furthermore let ρ be $\rho = \frac{z}{m\mu}$. Following results can be derived from the generalized system-level model, analogue to the M/M/m/∞/K Queue.

$$p_0 = \left[1 + M! \left(\sum_{k=1}^{min\{m,M\}} \frac{z^k}{(M-k)!k!\mu^k} + \frac{m^m}{m!} \sum_{k=m+1}^{min\{M,K\}} \frac{1}{(M-k)!} \rho^k \right) \right]^{-1} \tag{4.50}$$

$$p_k = \begin{cases} = p_0 \frac{M!z^k}{(M-k)!k!\mu^k} & \text{for } 0 < k \leq min\{m,M\} \\ = p_0 \frac{M!m^m}{(M-k)!m!} \rho^k & \text{for } m < k \leq min\{M,K\} \\ 0 & \text{else} \end{cases} \tag{4.51}$$

$$U = 1 - p_0 \tag{4.52}$$

$$X = \mu \left(\sum_{k=1}^{min\{m,M\}} kp_k + m \sum_{k=m+1}^{min\{M,K\}} p_k \right) \tag{4.53}$$

$$N = \sum_{k=1}^{min\{M,B\}} k \times p_k \tag{4.54}$$

Attention: By definition of capacity applies $K \geq m$! If $M \leq K$ the performance formulas are equal to the formulas of a M/M/m/∞/N queue.

4.2 Implementation

The Markovian Queue Solver is simply constructed and consists of the three main parts: *Queue*, *PerformanceSolver* and *MainMarkovianSolver*.

A *Queue* contains following performance relevant information of a resource:

- name as String
- capacity as Integer
- number of parallel servers as Integer
- workload type as Boolean (true if workload is closed, otherwise false)
- think time rate as BigDecimal
- population size as BigInteger

- arrival rate as BigDecimal

- service rate as BigDecimal

If a resource does not have a property e.g. closed workload type has no arrival rate, the corresponding value has to be set negative for example -1.

The *PerformanceSolver* solves performance metrics of a resource by using the analytical formulas. Since there are eight resources with different formulas, eight subclasses are necessary. Some of the implemented methods are:

- public abstract BigDecimal solveNrOfRequests()

- public abstract BigDecimal solveThroughput()

- public abstract BigDecimal solveUtilization()

- public BigDecimal solveResponseTime()

- public String solveAllToString()

For easier handling there is also the method *choosePerformanceSolver(Queue queue)* which checks the validity of the resource by the method *isQueueValid(Queue queue)* and selects the Markovian Queue Solver that matches the resource. A resource is solvable if:

- a (positive) service rate and at least one server exists

- the workload type is described correctly (open workload needs an arrival rate, closed workload needs a think time rate and a population size)

- capacity is at least equal (or bigger) than the number of parallel processing servers

- the arrival rate is smaller than the maximum possible service rate of the system, if the system has infinite population and no capacity limitations (for M/M/1 queue $\lambda < \mu$ and for M/M/m queue $\lambda < m\mu$, otherwise these queues are not solvable).

Finally, in the *MainMarkovianSolver* resources can be created and solved.

Formulas used in the Markovian Queue Solver were proved analytically. To ensure that they were implemented correctly, comparisons of performance results of all types of queues except the M/M/m/K/N queue (calculation of that queue is not available in the worksheet) were made with the excel-worksheet given in [MA98]. In addition, all eight queue types were tested by comparing the performance results with the simulation results of the JSIMGraph (cf. chapter 6.1).

5. Mapping Performance Formulas of Markovian Queues on Queueing Networks

This chapter discusses the applicability of basic queueing formulas to QNs. Figure 5.1 presents an overview. In chapter 3 we decided to restrict the type of QNs to product-form. All queues of the network have exponentially distributed arrival and service rates and the possible scheduling disciplines are FCFS, LCFS, PS or IS. These QNs meet the requirements of the BCMP theorem and are therefore product-form (cf. [Ste09] pp. 598).

The discussion of this chapter is organized in two main parts. In section 5.1 open QNs are in focus. We analyse how workload can be propagated to a certain queue of QNs with tandem topology (subsection 5.1.1) and with routing probabilities (subsection 5.1.2). In subsection 5.1.3 results are summarized. Workload propagation for further types of QN topologies are not mentioned in this paper. Section 5.2 deals with closed QNs. In subsection 5.2.1 we explain the difficulty of the application of basic queueing formulas on QNs with closed workload. In subsection 5.2.2 some algorithms for product-form QNs are shown, which can be used alternatively to get performance metrics of closed QNs.

Notation that will be used in this chapter:

- Queue q is the queue of interest to be examined regarding to performance metrics

- X_i is the throughput/departure rate of a queue i

- λ_i is the overall arrival rate of a queue i

- λ_{0i} is the arrival rate of requests from outside to node i

- μ_i is the service rate of a queue i

- p_{ji} is the routing probability that customers will arrive to queue i after service completion at queue j.

- p_{0i} is the routing probability that customers will arrive to queue i from an external source.

Note that λ_i and μ_i are not variable arrival and service rates any longer like they were used before in section 2.3.2 and in chapter 4.

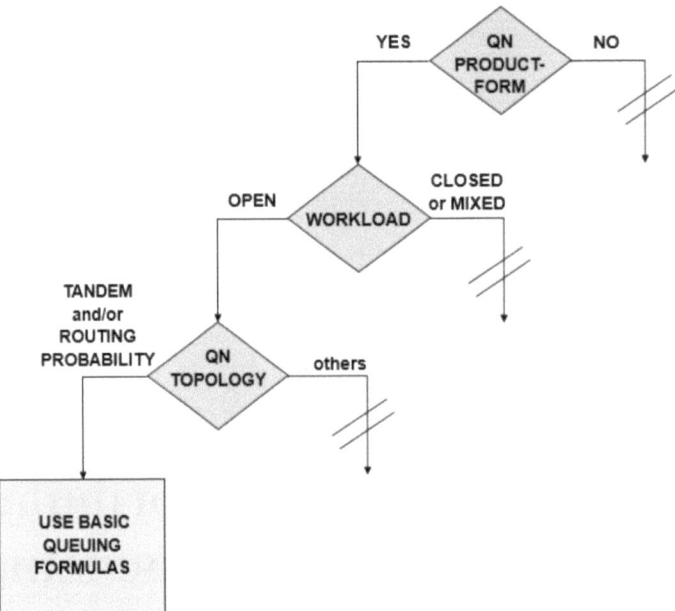

Figure 5.1: Flowchat describing when basic queueing formulas can be mapped on Queueing Networks

5.1 Open Queueing Networks

Determination of the propagated workload is easier in an open QN model than it is in a closed QN model because of two reasons. First, the workload is defined by a fixed arrival rate. Second, in open QNs there are clear starting points (one or more customer classes or external sources) and end points (points where customers leave the system). So the propagated workload of a queue q depends on all previous queues but not on successor queues.

Considered nodes of open QN's are of type M/M/1, M/M/m, M/M/1/K and M/M/m/K. First a simple QN with tandem topology is in focus (subsection 5.1.1), then routing probabilities are included (subsection 5.1.2). Finally in in the last section (subsection 5.1.3) generalized statements for open QN's are summarized.

5.1.1 Queueing Networks with Tandem Topology

A Queueing Network with tandem topology is an open QN, where all queues are connected in series. Customers arrive from an external source into the first queue with an arrival rate λ_{01} requests/sec. and after getting served, they visit the next queue with probability of 100% and so on, until all nodes are visited. Since we also want to consider nodes with capacity limitations, we have to expand the model slightly. So if a customer arrives in a queue with finite capacity that is fully exhausted, the customer leaves the QN without being served.

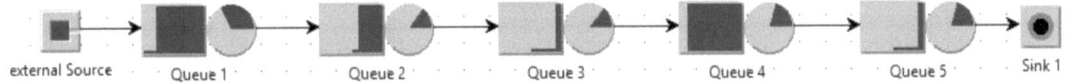

Figure 5.2: Open Queueing Network in tandem (from JSIMGraph)

To get the workload of an inner queue q, we need to determine throughputs of all previous queues. We start with the first queue, where the workload is known, propagate it to the second queue and so on, until queue q is reached. How to calculate departure rates depends on the type of node.

For a queue i without capacity limitations (M/M/1 and M/M/m queues) we have two possible scenarios. If the arrival rate is smaller than the highest possible service rate (for M/M/1 queue it is $\lambda_i < \mu_i$ and for M/M/m queue it is $\lambda_i < m\mu_i$), we know from the queue formulas of chapter 4 that $X_i = \lambda_i$, so the workload for the next queue does not change. If the arrival rate is equal or higher than the highest possible service rate, the queue will be totally busy and the departure rate will be the highest possible service rate: $X_i = \mu_i$ for a M/M/1 queue and $X_i = m\mu_i$ for a M/M/m queue. In that case only workload propagation is possible, performance metrics for queue i cannot be solved.

When we consider a QN with tandem topology consisting of many queues, the following can be deduced. If all previous nodes $i = 1, 2, ..., q - 1$ have infinite capacity and $\lambda_i \leq \mu_i$ (for M/M/1) or $\lambda_i \leq m\mu_i$ (for M/M/m), then $\lambda_q = \lambda_{01}$. In other words the arrival rate does not change. When the (propagated) arrival rate is higher than the highest possible service rate by at least one queue without capacity limitations, then $\lambda_q = min\{m\mu_i\} \leq \lambda_{01}$ for $i = 1, 2, ..., q - 1$. In this case a simulation may not be possible because of overflow of this queue. However when we use the analytical way, we can solve performance metrics of all nodes of the QN except that one.

For a queue i with capacity limitations there are no restrictions for the calculation of the throughput by the basic queue formula. In that case the formulas of chapter 4.1 can be used. Then the departure rate is $X_i \leq \lambda_i$ since some customers may leave the QN (if the capacity is fully exhausted).

5.1.2 Queueing Networks with Routing Probabilities

Similar to the central server network model for closed QNs, we can have an open QN with a central node, that schedules visits to other nodes (routing customers with probabilities to the next node). Note that in an open model customers do not return to the central node (as it is usually in a central server network). In figure 5.4 such a QN is presented.

To propagate workload and solve queues, we can use the relation of the exponential distributed arrival and service rates to the discrete Poisson random variable. If the interarrival times (times between successive arrivals of customers to a queue, for Markovian queues: $\frac{1}{\lambda}$) are exponentially distributed and independent with identical mean X, then the random variable that represents the number of customers that arrive in a fixed interval of time $[0,t]$ has a Poisson distribution with parameter $\alpha = \frac{t}{X}$ (see [BGdMT98] pp. 11). The arrival and service rates of Markovian queues meet the stated conditions (for which $t = 1$ sec.) so the following two important properties can be derived for them (cf. figure 5.3):

- When n independent Poisson processes with parameters λ_i ($i = 1, 2, ..., n$) merge into one process, then it is also a Poisson process with parameter $\lambda = \sum_{i=1}^{n} \lambda_i$.

- When a single Poisson process with parameter λ is decomposed into n independent processes in a way that customers are routed to the ith subprocess ($i = 1, 2, ..., n$) with probability p_i, then all subprocesses i are Poisson processes each with parameter $\lambda_i = p_i \times \lambda$.

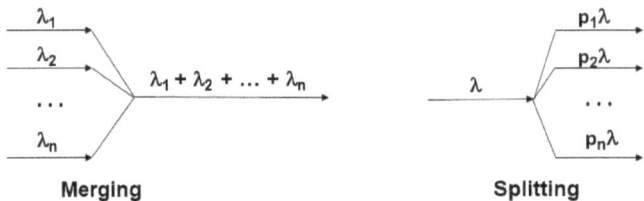

Merging   **Splitting**

Figure 5.3: Merging and splitting of Poisson Processes

From the first property we can conclude that if a node q has $n > 1$ predecessor nodes i ($i = q - 1, q - 2, ..., q - n$) with throughputs X_i, and $p_{i,q} = 1$ (e.g. Queue 6 in figure 5.4), then the arrival rate of queue q can be determined by the sum of all throuphputs of the previous nodes $\lambda_q = \sum_{i=1}^{n} X_i$. If the throughput of predecessor nodes i is splitted with routing probabilities $p_{i,q} < 1$ (like Queue 2-5 in figure 5.4), both properties can be used. The arrival rate of queue q is $\lambda_q = \sum_{i=1}^{n} p_{i,q} X_i$. In addition, if customers arrive from an external source then we have $\lambda_q = p_{0,q} \lambda_{0,q} + \sum_{i=1}^{n} p_{i,q} X_i$. In the same way, more customer classes can be included, since we can sum up all arrivals from external sources at node i. See also [BGdMT98] p.266 (note that our approach is more general and includes capacity limitations).

Further statements of workload propagation depending on the type of queue are analogue to section 5.1.1.

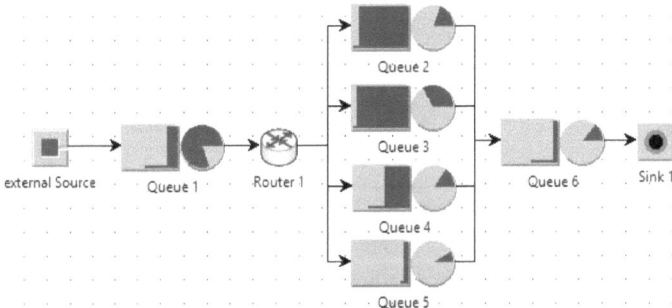

Figure 5.4: Open Queueing Network with routing probabilities (from JSIMGraph)

5.1.3 Summary

The acquired insights are to be summarized and generalized:

- To get workload of an inner queue q, we start with the first node, where the workload is known (from external sources) and propagate it to the next queue, till queue q is reached. How to calculate departure rates depends on the type of node.

- If a queue i is of type M/M/1 and $\lambda_i \geq \mu_i$ or of type M/M/m and $\lambda_i \geq m\mu_i$ only workload propagation is possible (see below), performance metrics for queue i cannot be solved, but performance metrics for other queues of the QN can be determined analytically.

- If a queue i is of type M/M/1 the departure rate is $X_i = min\{\lambda_i; \mu_i\}$. If a queue i is of type M/M/m the departure rate is $X_i = min\{\lambda_i; m\mu_i\}$.

- If a queue i is of type M/M/1/K or M/M/m/K the departure rate shall be computed by the regarding formula of chapter 4.1.

- The (inter-)arrival rate of a queue q can be computed by $\lambda_q = p_{0,q}\lambda_{0,q} + \sum_{i=1}^{n} p_{i,q}X_i$. With that rate basic queueing formulas can be used to calculate the performance metrics.

5.2 Closed Queueing Networks

Opportunities and difficulties of computing closed Queueing Networks are discussed in this section. In subsection 5.2.1 the possibility of mapping performance formulas of queues on QNs is figured out and in subsection 5.2.2 an overview of some algorithms for (closed) QNs is presented.

5.2.1 Discussion of Applicability of Basic Queueing Formulas

In closed Queueing Network models workload propagation is complex. One reason is that workload has a variable rate (defined by population size and think time) as we have seen in chapter 4, while in open models we use fixed arrival rates. Furthermore, requests in closed models have no external source where they arrive from (no starting point for workload propagation in equilibrium). Also customers do not leave the system but cycle in it, so interarrival times between nodes or departure rates of nodes are strongly correlated with each other, not only with the predecessor nodes. Departure rates in equilibrium are greatly influenced by the node with the lowest throughput (bottleneck node). But the QN size (number of nodes) affects different load scenarios and therefore the departure rates, too. Another factor are the service rates of all nodes and how close they are to the bottleneck node (the lower the service rates, the lower the throughput). Also there may be more influence parameters that are not considered here. Moreover the parameters, which act on departure rates, reinforce each other.

On the other hand we know that in a state equilibrium departure rates (throughputs) of nodes are fixed rates even if in the first step the system has variable rates. From [BGdMT98] page 266 we get the arrival rate for queues in closed models without capacity limitations: $\lambda_q = \sum_{i=1}^{n} p_{i,q}\lambda_i$ (since in closed models there is no external source, so $\lambda_{0,q} = 0$). This can be extended for nodes with finite capacity analogue to chapter 5.1 as follows: $\lambda_q = \sum_{i=1}^{n} p_{i,q}X_i$. But for workload propagation like it was done in open QNs, we have no starting point where this equation can be used. So basic queueing formulas cannot be used to propagate workload or to compute it.

If the throughput is known in equilibrium (e.g. determined by another method), the applicability of the basic formulas is unsatisfactory as well. Tests showed that we can only solve performance metrics of nodes that are not the bottleneck, e.g. by using formulas of M/M/1 or M/M/m queues (since in equilibrium the arrival rate is constant also for closed models). But the bottleneck, which is the node where the most interest lies in, cannot be solved by the formulas. Table 5.1 shows three tested QNs, which consist of five nodes (connected in series) and where the first node is the bottleneck node. In table 5.2 we can see that the deviation of the bottleneck node is very strong. For example the response time of QN 2 is almost seven times higher. Furthermore, when using algorithms or simulation to get the throughput, then all other performance metrics can be solved with that method, too. The use of the basic queueing formulas is unnecessary in that case.

Queue	Performance metrics of QN 1											
	Markovian Queue Solver				JSIMGraph				Difference			
	R	U	N	X	R	U	N	X	R	U	N	X
1	3,460	0,711	2,460	0,711	2,419	0,707	1,721	0,711	1,041	0,004	0,739	0,000
2	0,776	0,356	0,552	0,711	0,723	0,354	0,511	0,710	0,053	0,002	0,041	0,001
3	0,437	0,237	0,310	0,711	0,421	0,234	0,296	0,711	0,016	0,003	0,014	0,000
4	0,304	0,178	0,216	0,711	0,300	0,178	0,213	0,711	0,004	0,000	0,003	0,000
5	0,233	0,142	0,166	0,711	0,228	0,142	0,162	0,711	0,005	0,000	0,004	0,000

Queue	Performance metrics of QN 2											
	Markovian Queue Solver				JSIMGraph				Difference			
	R	U	N	X	R	U	N	X	R	U	N	X
1	1,044	0,633	1,034	0,990	8,135	0,986	7,851	0,990	-7,091	-0,353	-6,817	0,000
2	0,990	0,495	0,980	0,990	0,971	0,500	0,958	0,990	0,019	-0,005	0,022	0,000
3	0,498	0,330	0,493	0,990	0,493	0,332	0,489	0,990	0,005	-0,002	0,004	0,000
4	0,332	0,248	0,329	0,990	0,329	0,249	0,324	0,990	0,003	-0,001	0,005	0,000
5	0,249	0,198	0,247	0,990	0,248	0,198	0,243	0,990	0,001	0,000	0,004	0,000

Queue	Performance metrics of QN 3											
	Markovian Queue Solver				JSIMGraph				Difference			
	R	U	N	X	R	U	N	X	R	U	N	X
1	1,044	0,633	1,034	0,990	7,063	0,996	6,992	0,990	-6,019	-0,363	-5,958	0,000
2	0,990	0,495	0,980	0,990	0,974	0,497	0,963	0,990	0,016	-0,002	0,017	0,000
3	0,498	0,330	0,493	0,990	0,494	0,330	0,491	0,988	0,004	0,000	0,002	0,002
4	0,332	0,248	0,329	0,990	0,333	0,249	0,330	0,990	-0,001	-0,001	-0,001	0,000
5	0,249	0,198	0,247	0,990	0,251	0,199	0,248	0,990	-0,002	-0,001	-0,001	0,000

Table 5.2: Results of verified Queueing Networks with cycle topology

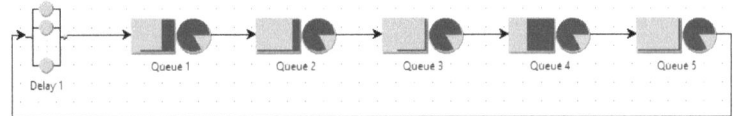

QN	popul.	z	Queue 1	Queue 2	Queue 3	Queue 4	Queue 5
			M/M/1	M/M/1	M/M/1	M/M/1	M/M/1
1	10	0,1	$\mu = 1,0$	$\mu = 2,0$	$\mu = 3,0$	$\mu = 4,0$	$\mu = 5,0$
2	20	0,1	$\mu = 1,0$	$\mu = 2,0$	$\mu = 3,0$	$\mu = 4,0$	$\mu = 5,0$
3	10	1	$\mu = 1,0$	$\mu = 2,0$	$\mu = 3,0$	$\mu = 4,0$	$\mu = 5,0$

Table 5.1: Verified Queueing Networks with cycle topology

5.2.2 Overview of Algorithms for Product-Form Queueing Networks

Product-form queueing networks for open models were introduced by Jackson and for closed models by Gordon and Newell. Their results were extended in 1975 by Baskett, Chandy, Muntz and Palacios. They defined the most famous class of product-form QNs: the BCMP queueing networks. Performance metrics for open, closed and mixed QNs with multiple customer classes and different scheduling disciplines and service time distributions can be calculated for that class of QNs by computational algorithms. Requirements for the BCMP queueing networks (e.g. scheduling disciplines, job classes) can be found in [Jai90] p. 551 or in [BGdMT98] p. 300. The most important algorithms for closed models are the Convolution Algorithm and the Mean Value Analysis (MVA).

The *Convolution algorithm*, also referred to as Buzen's algorithm, is one of the first for analysing closed product-form QNs. The complete set of marginal probabilities of each node can be computed with it. By an iterative technique the so called normalization constant is determined and with that constant all performance measures can be derived. The Convolution algorithm is more complex than the MVA, but some more information such as the distribution or variance of queue lengths and response times can be computed (e.g. probability of a two-disk computer system, that both disks are busy at the same time). More details can be found in [BGdMT98] pp. 313 or [Jai90] pp. 593.

Mean Value Analysis (MVA) is a recursive method, where mean values of the performance metrics can be determined directly (without the normalization constant). The algorithm is based on the property of closed product-form QNs, that "the stationary distribution observed by a customer arriving at a node of the network is equal to the stationary distribution of customers in the same network with one fewer customer" (arrival theorem from [Ste09] p. 582) and on Little' law ("mean number in the system = arrival rate x mean response time" [Jai90] p. 513). The arrival theorem is necessary to compute the average response time R_i at each node i and Little's law is necessary to compute the overall throughput X and the mean number of customers N_i at each node. The recursive process begins by the equation $N_i(0) = 0$ since in a system with zero customers the number of customers at each node is also zero. Next response time $R_i(1)$ for all nodes i with one customer can be calculated and with that the overall throughput for one customer $X(1)$. When knowing $R_i(1)$ and $X(1)$ average numbers of customers $N_i(1)$ for all nodes i and one customer in the system can be solved. Then the second round begins by calculating $R_i(2)$ (two customers in system), where $N_i(1)$ is used. This process is continued until population size is reached. The normalization constant can additionally be computed with MVA. For more details see [BGdMT98] pp. 326 or [Jai90] pp. 570.

The calculation of product-form networks with multiple customer classes is more difficult. Convolution and MVA algorithms have been extended for that networks, but their costs grow exponentially with the number of customer classes (cf. [Bal00]). Therefore further algorithms have been developed, e.g. *Recursion by Chain Algorithm* (Recal) (cf. [BGdMT98] pp.360), *Mean Value Analysis by Chain* or *Distribution Analysis by Chain* (DAC). Their computational costs are polynomial with the number of customer classes, but exponential in the number of nodes ([Bal00]). There are even more algorithms that are not metioned here but are well suited for networks with certain characteristics (e.g. LBANC for large number of jobs but small number of nodes or CCNC for limited storage spaces).

Furthermore there is an analytical procedure to decompose large Queueing Networks: the *flow equivalent server* (FES) method, (also called flow equivalent center FEC). FES is based on Norton's theorem from electric circuit theory, which is also applicable to QNs (shown by Chandy, Herzog and Woo in 1975). The theorem states that "the reduced system has the same behaviour as the original network" (from [BGdMT98] p. 368) if one or more queues were selected and all other combined into a FES. This method is a great tool to analyse various alternatives for a specific node and is also a foundation for approximate solution methods of more general non-product form QNs. The basic FES algorithm consists of three main steps. First, a shortened model has to be created. Therefore a queue or a set of queues of interest are chosen and their service times are set to zero. Next, the service rates of the aggregated subnetwork need to be computed. These service rates are the throughputs of the shorted model depending on the number of jobs in the system. So the aggregated subnetwork is load-dependent (variable service rates), described as a function of the numbers of M jobs. For example MVA or Convolution algorithm can be used to work out the throughput of the shortened model for $1, 2, ..., M$ jobs. In the last step, the reduced model can be considered and performance metrics can be solved e.g. by Convolution or MVA. For more details see [BGdMT98] pp. 368 or [Jai90] pp. 608.

6. Evaluation

In this chapter the Markovian Queue Solver is tested. On the one hand, a practical comparison is carried out between performance metrics, which are ascertained by the Markovian Queue Solver and a simulation with the JSIMGraph tool. The aim is to evaluate when and why deviations occur and how strong they are. In section 6.1 single queue models and in section 6.2 Queueing Network models with tandem topology are examined. On the other hand we want to find out if and how much faster the analytical method is in contrast to the simulation method. This is done in section 6.3. Chosen scheduling discipline of queues in JSIMGraph is Processor Sharing (PS), capacity limitations and number of servers are also considered in the simulation. More details of JSIMGraph and which parameters are used there can be found in chapter 3.

6.1 Performance Measures of Queues

Performance metrics of open models with a single server with or without capacity limitations (M/M/1 and M/M/1/K queues) and closed models with a single server and without capacity limitations (M/M/1/∞/N queues) determined by the simulation are very close to results of the Markovian Queue Solver (deviations mostly under 1%, see table 6.1). Only for small service rates the response time varies slightly more, probably due to rounding values of the implemented formulas (deviations under 5%).

We also get minimal deviation (under 3%, mostly under 1%) by comparing response time, throughput and number of requests of multiple server queues (M/M/m, M/M/m/K and M/M/m/∞/N queues). However, the utilization rates are very different, i.e. in some cases more than 200% higher when using the analytical solver (cf. table 6.2). The reason for this seems to be a different definition of the utilization. Formulas are based on the assumption that multiple server queues are busy when at least one server is busy. But such a queue is only busy for a fraction when using JSIMGraph. If we compare performance results of the simulation tool using a (load independent) M/M/m queue with results of the analytical solver using a M/M/1 queue with a service rate that is the maximum possible service rate of the M/M/m queue ($\mu_{M/M/1} = m\mu_{M/M/5}$), the utilization is almost the same (deviations under 3%), but number of requests and response time vary up to 20% (cf. table 6.3)! The same is the case when comparing results of a M/M/m queue computed by the Markovian Queue Solver and a M/M/1 queue worked out by the JSIMGraph, that is load dependent (here all m values must be entered, $\mu_1 = \mu, \mu_2 = 2\mu, ..., \mu_m = m\mu$). The deviations of the

| Input parameter | | Performance metrics of M/M/1 queues | | | | | | | | | | | |
| λ | μ | Markovian Queue Solver | | | | JSIMGraph | | | | Difference | | | |
		R	U	N	X	R	U	N	X	R	U	N	X
0,5	2	0,667	0,250	0,333	0,500	0,670	0,248	0,334	0,497	-0,003	0,002	-0,001	0,003
0,5	4	0,286	0,125	0,143	0,500	0,284	0,125	0,143	0,501	0,002	0,000	0,000	-0,001
2	2,5	2,000	0,800	4,000	2,000	2,016	0,799	4,034	1,998	-0,016	0,001	-0,034	0,002
2	4	0,500	0,500	1,000	2,000	0,498	0,498	0,997	1,988	0,002	0,002	0,003	0,012
8	9	1,000	0,889	8,000	8,000	1,020	0,913	8,133	8,035	-0,020	-0,024	-0,133	-0,035

| Input parameter | | Performance metrics of M/M/1/20 queues | | | | | | | | | | | |
| λ | μ | Markovian Queue Solver | | | | JSIMGraph | | | | Difference | | | |
		R	U	N	X	R	U	N	X	R	U	N	X
0,5	0,3	61,670	1,000	18,500	0,300	61,881	1,000	18,501	0,300	-0,211	0,000	-0,001	0,000
2	1	19,000	1,000	19,000	1,000	18,911	1,000	19,018	1,004	0,089	0,000	-0,018	-0,004
2	2	5,250	0,952	10,000	1,905	5,244	0,952	10,023	1,899	0,006	0,000	-0,023	0,006
2	4	0,500	0,500	1,000	2,000	0,501	0,502	1,008	2,003	-0,001	-0,002	-0,008	-0,003
8	4	4,750	1,000	19,000	4,000	4,744	1,000	19,020	4,003	0,006	0,000	-0,020	-0,003
8	8	1,313	0,952	10,000	7,620	1,297	0,948	9,972	7,649	0,016	0,004	0,028	-0,029
8	10	0,477	0,799	3,805	7,981	0,456	0,800	3,806	7,996	0,021	-0,001	-0,001	-0,015

| Input parameter | | Performance metrics of M/M/1/∞/10 queues | | | | | | | | | | | |
| z | μ | Markovian Queue Solver | | | | JSIMGraph | | | | Difference | | | |
		R	U	N	X	R	U	N	X	R	U	N	X
0,5	0,3	31,333	1,000	9,400	0,300	31,226	1,000	9,393	0,301	0,107	0,000	0,007	-0,001
0,5	1	8,000	1,000	8,000	1,000	7,939	1,000	7,972	1,006	0,061	0,000	0,028	-0,006
0,5	5	0,546	0,785	2,146	3,927	0,537	0,783	2,132	3,933	0,009	0,002	0,014	-0,006
1	5	1,037	0,982	5,092	4,908	1,045	0,983	5,117	4,882	-0,008	-0,001	-0,025	0,026
2	2	4,500	1,000	9,000	2,000	4,485	1,000	8,989	1,996	0,015	0,000	0,011	0,004

Table 6.1: Compared performance metrics of single server queues

utilizations are under 2% but for the response time and number of requests they are up to 70% (cf. table 6.3).

| Input parameter | | Performance metrics of M/M/5 queues | | | | | | | | | | | |
| λ | μ | Markovian Queue Solver | | | | JSIMGraph - load independent | | | | Difference | | | |
		R	U	N	X	R	U	N	X	R	U	N	X
0,5	0,3	3,364	0,812	1,682	0,500	3,354	0,333	1,678	0,498	0,010	0,479	0,004	0,002
0,5	1	1,000	0,393	0,500	0,500	1,001	0,099	0,467	0,5	-0,001	0,294	0,033	0,000
2	0,5	3,108	0,987	6,216	2,000	3,107	0,79	6,22	1,996	0,001	0,197	-0,004	0,004
2	1	1,020	0,866	2,040	2,000	1,015	0,399	2,036	2,01	0,005	0,467	0,004	-0,010
8	2	0,777	0,987	6,216	8,000	0,781	0,807	6,218	8,012	-0,004	0,180	-0,002	-0,012
8	4	0,255	0,866	2,040	8,000	0,255	0,403	2,056	7,994	0,000	0,463	-0,016	0,006

| Input parameter | | Performance metrics of M/M/5/20 queues | | | | | | | | | | | |
| λ | μ | Markovian Queue Solver | | | | JSIMGraph | | | | Difference | | | |
		R	U	N	X	R	U	N	X	R	U	N	X
0,5	0,3	3,364	0,812	1,682	0,500	3,353	0,333	1,670	0,499	0,011	0,479	0,012	0,001
2	0,1	39,333	1,000	19,667	0,500	39,250	1,000	19,664	0,502	0,083	0,000	0,003	-0,002
2	0,4	5,927	0,999	11,210	1,892	5,942	0,949	11,228	1,884	-0,015	0,050	-0,018	0,008
2	0,8	1,315	0,920	2,630	2,000	1,328	0,501	2,657	1,997	-0,013	0,419	-0,027	0,003
2	1,6	0,627	0,714	1,253	2,000	0,628	0,249	1,250	2,013	-0,001	0,465	0,003	-0,013
2	3	0,333	0,487	0,667	2,000	0,334	0,133	0,665	1,995	-0,001	0,354	0,002	0,005
8	1	3,668	1,000	18,337	4,999	3,650	1,000	18,347	5,011	0,018	0,000	-0,010	-0,012
8	4	0,255	0,866	2,040	8,000	0,260	0,408	2,082	8,052	-0,005	0,458	-0,042	-0,052
8	8	0,125	0,632	1,001	8,000	0,125	0,200	1,002	8,003	0,000	0,432	-0,001	-0,003
8	10	0,100	0,551	0,800	8,000	0,100	0,160	0,801	8,032	0,000	0,391	-0,001	-0,032

| Input parameter | | Performance metrics of M/M/5/∞/10 queues | | | | | | | | | | | |
| z | μ | Markovian Queue Solver | | | | JSIMGraph | | | | Difference | | | |
		R	U	N	X	R	U	N	X	R	U	N	X
0,5	0,3	4,803	1,000	7,060	1,470	4,868	0,981	7,078	1,461	-0,065	0,019	-0,018	0,009
0,5	1	1,046	0,983	3,434	3,283	1,048	0,661	3,423	3,279	-0,002	0,322	0,011	0,004
0,5	5	0,200	0,614	0,909	4,545	0,201	0,183	0,916	4,537	-0,001	0,431	-0,007	0,008
1	5	0,200	0,839	1,670	8,330	0,201	0,334	1,676	8,367	-0,001	0,505	-0,006	-0,037
2	2	0,610	0,999	5,496	9,008	0,605	0,898	5,476	9,050	0,005	0,101	0,020	-0,042
8	5	0,285	1,000	6,948	24,419	0,285	0,976	6,935	24,427	0,000	0,024	0,013	-0,008
8	10	0,114	0,998	4,778	41,775	0,114	0,832	4,759	41,618	0,000	0,166	0,019	0,157

Table 6.2: Compared performance metrics of multiple server queues

Input parameter		Performance metrics													
		Markovian Queue Solver - M/M/5				JSIMGraph - M/M/1 load dependent				Difference			
λ	μ	R	U	N	X	R	U	N	X	R	U	N	X
0,5	0,3	3,364	0,812	1,682	0,500	3,577	0,802	1,932	0,5	-0,213	0,010	-0,250	0,000
0,5	1	1,000	0,393	0,500	0,500	1,068	0,389	0,529	0,5	-0,068	0,004	-0,029	0,000
2	0,5	3,108	0,987	6,216	2,000	3,856	0,978	7,944	2,003	-0,748	0,009	-1,728	-0,003
2	1	1,020	0,866	2,040	2,000	1,194	0,846	2,383	1,999	-0,174	0,020	-0,343	0,001
8	2	0,777	0,987	6,216	8,000	0,964	0,98	7,732	8,036	-0,187	0,007	-1,516	-0,036
8	4	0,255	0,866	2,040	8,000	0,3	0,85	2,415	8,016	-0,045	0,016	-0,375	-0,016

Input parameter		Performance metrics													
		Markovian Queue Solver - M/M/1 with service rate of 5*μ				JSIMGraph - M/M/5 load independent				Difference			
λ	μ	R	U	N	X	R	U	N	X	R	U	N	X
0,5	0,3	1,000	0,333	0,500	0,500	3,354	0,333	1,678	0,498	-2,354	0,000	-1,178	0,002
0,5	1	0,222	0,100	0,111	0,500	1,001	0,099	0,467	0,5	-0,779	0,001	-0,356	0,000
2	0,5	2,000	0,800	4,000	2,000	3,107	0,79	6,22	1,996	-1,107	0,010	-2,220	0,004
2	1	0,333	0,400	0,667	2,000	1,015	0,399	2,036	2,01	-0,682	0,001	-1,369	-0,010
8	2	0,500	0,800	4,000	8,000	0,781	0,807	6,218	8,012	-0,281	-0,007	-2,218	-0,012
8	4	0,083	0,400	0,667	8,000	0,255	0,403	2,056	7,994	-0,172	-0,003	-1,389	0,006

Table 6.3: Compared performance metrics of multiple vs. single server queues

At least we examine closed queue models with capacity limitations. The queue models of interest are queues where the capacity is exceeded. In the other case, where capacity size is smaller than population size, we get results that are equal to those with infinite capacity. All four performance metrics differ significantly in that case, when comparing the analytical Solver with JSIMGraph (deviations over 5%, up to 500%, see table 6.4). This is based on a different model understanding. In the specialized system-level model formulas can be developed because of the steady-state assumption. If the model has finite capacity, requests are refused to the queue when capacity is exceeded, but the population size does not change. However in the first step of the simulation all N requests move to the queue with capacity of K, but $(N - K)$ requests leave the closed system completely. So in the next step, we have a queue that is equal with one that has a population size of K. It is not surprising that the results of the JSIMGraph are very close to those of the Markovian Queue Solver, where a queue is used with population size of K instead of N (deviations under 5 % mostly under 1%, see table 6.5).

Input parameter		Performance metrics of M/M/1/5/20 queues													
		Markovian Queue Solver				JSIMGraph				Difference			
z	μ	R	U	N	X	R	U	N	X	R	U	N	X
0,5	0,3	16,537	1,000	4,961	0,300	14,537	1,000	4,402	0,298	2,000	0,000	0,559	0,002
0,5	1	4,860	1,000	4,860	1,000	3,182	0,963	3,061	0,964	1,678	0,037	1,799	0,036
0,5	5	0,791	0,977	3,887	4,886	0,296	0,438	0,647	2,188	0,495	0,539	3,240	2,698
1	5	0,917	0,994	4,577	4,994	0,399	0,713	1,421	3,586	0,518	0,281	3,156	1,408
2	2	2,467	1,000	4,934	2,000	2,000	0,997	4,014	2,005	0,467	0,003	0,920	-0,005

Table 6.4: Compared performance metrics of a closed model and finite capacity

Input parameter		Performance metrics													
		Markovian Queue Solver M/M/1/5/5				JSIMGraph M/M/1/5/20				Difference			
z	μ	R	U	N	X	R	U	N	X	R	U	N	X
0,5	0,3	14,673	1,000	4,400	0,300	14,537	1,000	4,402	0,298	0,136	0,000	-0,002	0,002
0,5	1	3,190	0,963	3,073	0,963	3,182	0,963	3,061	0,964	0,008	0,000	0,012	-0,001
0,5	5	0,293	0,436	0,640	2,180	0,296	0,438	0,647	2,188	-0,003	-0,002	-0,007	-0,008
1	5	0,398	0,715	1,424	3,576	0,399	0,713	1,421	3,586	-0,001	0,002	0,003	-0,010
2	2	2,008	0,997	4,003	1,994	2,000	0,997	4,014	2,005	0,008	0,000	-0,011	-0,011

Table 6.5: Compared performance metrics of a closed model, but different finite capacity

In the table below results are summarized. Symbol for negligible deviations up to 5%

between appropriate performance results of Markovian Queue Solver and JSIMGraph is ✓, while for bigger deviations (more than 5%) x is used.

queue characteristics	performance metrics				
	R	U	N	X	all
M/M/1	✓	✓	✓	✓	✓
M/M/m	✓	x	✓	✓	x
M/M/1/K	✓	✓	✓	✓	✓
M/M/m/K	✓	x	✓	✓	x
M/M/1/∞/N	✓	✓	✓	✓	✓
M/M/m/∞/N	✓	x	✓	✓	x
M/M/1/K/N	x	x	x	x	x
M/M/m/K/N	x	x	x	x	x

6.2 Performance Measures of Queueing Networks

In chapter 5.1 the analyzed open QNs had tandem topology and routing probabilities. Therefore we compare performance measures of open QNs that are connected in series (tandem) and afterwards some QNs with routing probabilities are considered. Computing performance metrics of closed QNs with basic queueing formulas is not recommended (cf. chapter 5.2) and hence will not be tested. Compared performance metrics are: average response time R, average number of requests N and average throughput X each of a queue q. Average utilization U is not contemplated because of the great difference between Markovian Queue Solver and JSIMGraph for multiple server queues (see section 6.1).

Table 6.6 shows some tested QNs consist of five nodes in tandem and an external arrival rate λ_1. The last column contains the propagated arrival rate of queue five (all λ_5's are calculated with Markovian Queue Solver). When all nodes of the QN have infinite capacity (QN 1 to 4), then $\lambda_5 = \lambda_1$. QN 5 to 8 have queues with finite capacity and the (maximum possible) service rates are smaller than the arrival rates (nodes are fully loaded). Customers leave the system when the capacity is fully exhausted, so $\lambda_5 < \lambda_1$. For example the propagated arrival rates of QN 7 are: $\lambda_1 = 8 \le \lambda_2 = 5.874 \le \lambda_3 = 3,809 \le \lambda_4 = 3.685 \le \lambda_5 = 3,685$. A comparison (Markovian Queue Solver versus JSIMGraph) of the performance metrics of queue five can be found in table 6.7.

QN	λ_1	Queue 1	Queue 2	Queue 3	Queue 4	Queue 5	λ_5
		M/M/1	M/M/1	M/M/1	M/M/1	M/M/1	
1	0,5	μ = 0,7	μ = 1,0	μ = 0,9	μ = 2,0	μ = 0,6	0,5
2	0,5	μ = 0,7	μ = 0,5	μ = 0,9	μ = 2,0	μ = 1,0	0,5
		M/M/3	M/M/5	M/M/2	M/M/6	M/M/3	
3	1	μ = 0,7	μ = 1,0	μ = 0,9	μ = 2,0	μ = 0,6	1
4	1	μ = 0,5	μ = 0,5	μ = 0,5	μ = 0,5	μ = 0,5	1
5		M/M/1	M/M/5	M/M/1/20	M/M/1/10	M/M/1/20	
	1	μ = 1,5	μ = 0,5	μ = 0,5	μ = 0,9	μ = 1,0	0,499
		M/M/3/10	M/M/5/5	M/M/5/10	M/M/3/20	M/M/3/20	
6	1	μ = 0,1	μ = 0,1	μ = 0,1	μ = 0,1	μ = 0,1	0,263
7	8	μ = 2,0	μ = 1,0	μ = 1,0	μ = 2,0	μ = 2,0	3,685
8	1	μ = 2,0	μ = 3,0	μ = 0,1	μ = 2,0	μ = 3,0	0,498

Table 6.6: Verified Queueing Networks with tandem topology

QN	Performance metrics of Queue 5								
	Markovian Queue Solver			JSIMGraph			Difference		
	R	N	X	R	N	X	R	N	X
1	10,000	5,000	0,500	9,931	5,069	0,503	0,069	-0,069	-0,003
2	2,000	1,000	0,500	1,991	0,988	0,501	0,009	0,012	-0,001
3	2,041	2,041	1,000	2,055	2,048	1,003	-0,014	-0,007	-0,003
4	2,889	2,889	1,000	2,906	2,920	1,003	-0,017	-0,031	-0,003
5	1,996	0,996	0,499	1,962	0,994	0,497	0,034	0,002	0,002
6	25,225	6,554	0,260	24,736	6,461	0,261	0,489	0,093	-0,001
7	0,661	2,435	3,685	0,636	2,383	3,735	0,025	0,052	-0,050
8	0,333	0,166	0,498	0,334	0,166	0,501	-0,001	0,000	-0,003

Table 6.7: Results of verified Queueing Networks with tandem topology

Next, tests of QNs with routing probabilities are presented. QNs consist of six nodes as it is shown in figure 6.1. More details (queue type, service rate, external arrival rate, probability) of the tested QNs can be found in table 6.1. Queues of interest are those where the throughput of the previous queue is splitted and are those where the arrival rate is merged from previous queues. So in the two last columns of the table the propagated workload of queue three and queue six is inserted (computed by the Markovian Queue Solver). Tested QNs consist of queues with and without capacity limitations and with a single as well as with multiple servers. Compared performance results of queue three and queue six can be found in table 6.9.

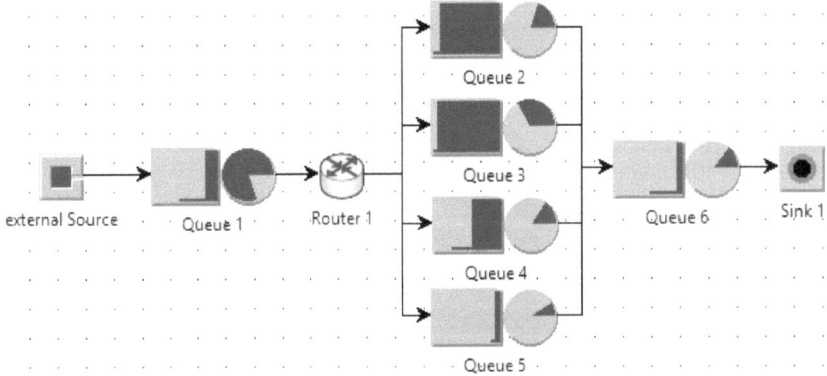

Figure 6.1: Open Queueing Network with routing probabilities (from JSIMGraph)

QN	λ_1	Queue 1	Queue 2	Queue 3	Queue 4	Queue 5	Queue 6	λ_3	λ_6
1	8	M/M/1 $\mu = 10$	M/M/5 $\mu = 0,5$ p $= 0,25$	M/M/3 $\mu = 1$; p $= 0,25$	M/M/5 $\mu = 0,4$; p $= 0,25$	M/M/1 $\mu = 2$; p $= 0,25$	M/M/5 $\mu = 2$	2,00	8,00
2	8	$\mu = 10$	$\mu = 1$; p $= 0,4$	$\mu = 1$; p $= 0,3$	$\mu = 0,4$; p $= 0,2$	$\mu = 1$; p $= 0,1$	$\mu = 2$	2,40	8,00
3	8	M/M/1 $\mu = 10$	M/M/5/20 $\mu = 0,4$; p $= 0,25$	M/M/3/20 $\mu = 0,6$; p $= 0,25$	M/M/5/40 $\mu = 0,3$; p $= 0,25$	M/M/3/40 $\mu = 0,6$; p $= 0,25$	M/M/5/20 $\mu = 1,5$	2,00	6,96
4	8	$\mu = 10$	$\mu = 0,6$; p $= 0,4$	$\mu = 0,6$; p $= 0,3$	$\mu = 0,3$; p $= 0,2$	$\mu = 0,2$; p $= 0,1$	$\mu = 1$	2,40	6,80
5	8	M/M/1 $\mu = 10$	M/M/5 $\mu = 0,5$ p $= 0,25$	M/M/3 $\mu = 1$; p $= 0,25$	M/M/5/40 $\mu = 0,3$; p $= 0,25$	M/M/3/40 $\mu = 0,6$; p $= 0,25$	M/M/5/20 $\mu = 1$	2,00	7,30
6	8	M/M/1 $\mu = 10$	M/M/5/20 $\mu = 0,6$; p $= 0,4$	M/M/3/20 $\mu = 0,6$; p $= 0,3$	M/M/5 $\mu = 0,4$; p $= 0,2$	M/M/3 $\mu = 1$; p $= 0,1$	M/M/5 $\mu = 2$	2,40	7,11

Table 6.8: Verified Queueing Networks with routing probabilities

| QN | Performance metrics of Queue 3 | | | | | | | | |
| | Markovian Queue Solver | | | JSIMGraph | | | Difference | | |
	R	N	X	R	N	X	R	N	X
1	1,444	2,889	2,000	1,448	2,883	1,991	-0,004	0,006	0,009
2	2,079	4,989	2,400	2,112	5,003	2,411	-0,033	-0,014	-0,011
3	7,784	13,791	1,772	7,675	13,566	1,777	0,109	0,225	-0,005
4	9,492	17,066	1,798	9,478	17,168	1,805	0,014	-0,102	-0,007
5	1,444	2,889	2,000	1,445	2,895	2,005	-0,001	-0,006	-0,005
6	9,492	17,066	1,798	9,643	17,213	1,798	-0,151	-0,147	0,000

| QN | Performance metrics of Queue 6 | | | | | | | | |
| | Markovian Queue Solver | | | JSIMGraph | | | Difference | | |
	R	N	X	R	N	X	R	N	X
1	0,777	6,216	8,000	0,769	6,140	7,969	0,008	0,076	0,031
2	0,777	6,216	8,000	0,780	6,235	8,017	-0,003	-0,019	-0,017
3	1,341	9,093	6,781	1,346	9,123	6,789	-0,005	-0,030	-0,008
4	3,462	17,289	4,994	3,470	17,380	4,973	-0,008	-0,091	0,021
5	3,570	17,841	4,998	3,623	17,937	4,944	-0,053	-0,096	0,054
6	0,637	4,529	7,111	0,642	4,531	7,085	-0,005	-0,002	0,026

Table 6.9: Results of verified Queueing Networks with routing probabilities

All performance results of QNs with tandem topology as well as with routing probabilities are close to one another. Deviations of all tested QNs were minimal, smaller than 4% (most of them where smaller than 2%). They can be explained by inaccuracies due to mathematical rounds when using the analytical procedure or by the selected confidence interval of the simulation.

6.3 Savings in Computational Costs

A great advantage of analytical procedures compared to simulations are savings on computational costs. In the following, examples are used to check whether and how much faster results can be achieved with the Markovian Queue Solver by comparison with JSIMGraph. In this respect, individual open and closed queueing models are considered as well as open Queueing Network models consisting of three and ten nodes.

The time analysis initially concerns queueing models. All four performance metrics of queues were queried and the time required for this was measured. Queues with open workload with finite and infinite capacity were tested as well as queues with closed workload. More details about the queues and the needed time to compute performance measures can be found in table 6.10. In figure 6.2 the results are compared graphically. For M/M/1 queues, the formulas are simple and therefore very fast (0,0 milliseconds). And for the other queues the Markovian Queue Solver was 27 to 47 times faster than the simulation!

| Queue | Input parameter | | | | Time in sec. | |
	type	λ	μ	z	MQS	JSIMGraph
1	M/M/1	10	20	-	0,000	3,687
2	M/M/1	10	11	-	0,000	8,391
3	M/M/1/20	10	8	-	0,063	2,928
4	M/M/1/∞/20	10	40	1	0,094	2,552
5	M/M/1/∞/20	10	10	1	0,094	3,929

Table 6.10: Verified Queues with open and closed workload

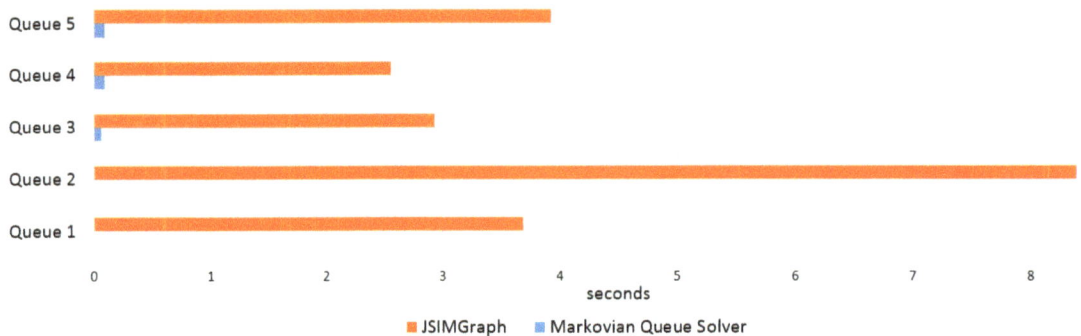

Figure 6.2: Required time for solving performance metrics of Queues

Simple open QNs with tandem topology, that consist of three nodes, are chosen next. Some QNs have infinite capacity queues only, others have nodes with finite capacity. More details of the QNs can be found in table 6.12, where λ_1 is the external arrival rate. To get results from the analytical solver we created the mentioned QNs by using an array of queues in Java (since Markovian Queue Solver has no meta-model for QNs). The external arrival rate was set into Queue 1, the arrival rates of the other queues were set to -1. Then we started the Markovian Queue Solver. There the specific workload/the respective arrival rates for all queues were calculated and set into the queues first (workload propagation) and afterwards all four performance metrics for all queues were queried (by a loop). It was confirmed that the analytical procedure is much faster than the simulation. Again, the Markovian Queue Solver is the fastest on QNs consisting of nodes without capacity limitations, since the formulas are simple (0.0 milliseconds). For the other QNs the analytical Solver was 108 to 243 times faster than JSMIGraph!

| QN | λ_1 | Input parameter | | | Time in sec. | |
		Queue 1	Queue 2	Queue 3	MQS	JSIMGraph
		M/M/1	M/M/1	M/M/1		
1	10	$\mu = 20{,}0$	$\mu = 30{,}0$	$\mu = 20{,}0$	0,000	5,345
2	10	$\mu = 20{,}0$	$\mu = 15{,}0$	$\mu = 11{,}0$	0,000	17,497
3	10	$\mu = 11{,}0$	$\mu = 11{,}0$	$\mu = 11{,}0$	0,000	17,752
		M/M/1	M/M/1	M/M/1 /20		
4	10	$\mu = 11{,}0$	$\mu = 11{,}0$	$\mu = 8{,}0$	0,078	18,915
		M/M/1 /20	M/M/1 /20	M/M/1 /20		
5	10	$\mu = 10{,}0$	$\mu = 11{,}0$	$\mu = 8{,}0$	0,109	11,749

Table 6.11: Verified Queueing Networks

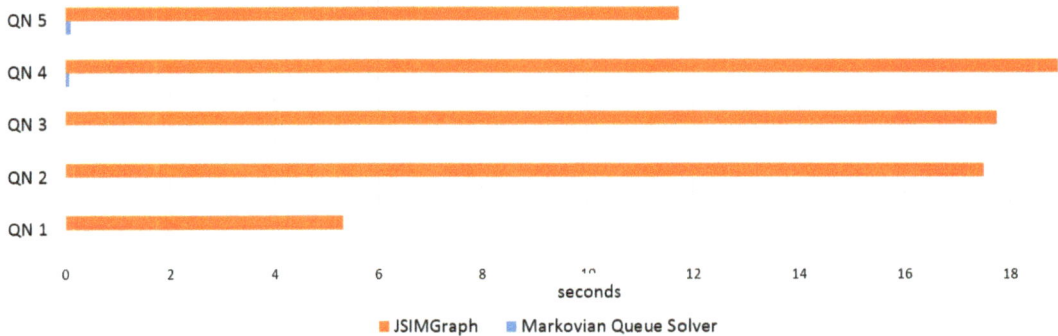

Figure 6.3: Required time for solving performance metrics of QNs

Last, a bigger open QN with tandem topology and ten nodes (with and without capacity limitations) and an external arrival rate of $\lambda_1 = 10$ is tested. More details can be found in table 6.12 below (note that performance metrics of Queue 3 cannot be solved analytically, since arrival rate = service rate, but workload propagation is possible). All four queue specific performance metrics are computed each for Queue i, $i = 2, 4, 6, 8, 10$ by the Markovian Queue Solver and by JSIMGraph. Other structures and sequences of the test are analogue to those QNs with three nodes. As expected, both solvers need more time for this QN then for a smaller one with three nodes. Nevertheless the Markovian Queue Solver is very fast. While the simulation lasted about 35 seconds (35.468 seconds), the analytical method was just 0.174 seconds (204 times faster)! Figure 6.4 illustrates the difference.

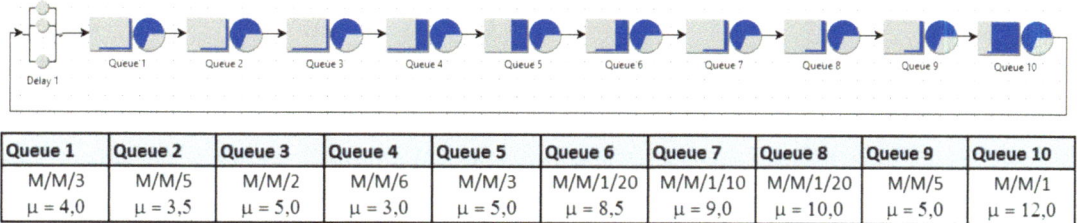

Queue 1	Queue 2	Queue 3	Queue 4	Queue 5	Queue 6	Queue 7	Queue 8	Queue 9	Queue 10
M/M/3	M/M/5	M/M/2	M/M/6	M/M/3	M/M/1/20	M/M/1/10	M/M/1/20	M/M/5	M/M/1
$\mu = 4,0$	$\mu = 3,5$	$\mu = 5,0$	$\mu = 3,0$	$\mu = 5,0$	$\mu = 8,5$	$\mu = 9,0$	$\mu = 10,0$	$\mu = 5,0$	$\mu = 12,0$

Table 6.12: Verified Queueing Network with tandem topology

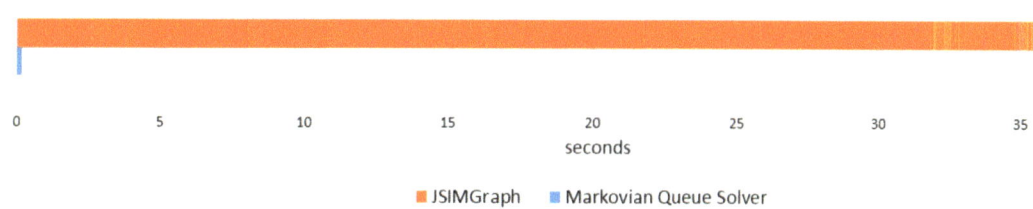

Figure 6.4: Required time for solving performance metrics of a tandem QN with ten nodes

For simulation as well as for the analytical procedure the following applies in general: the more nodes the QN has, the more time the solution requires. Moreover, the simulation takes longer the more the system is loaded, e.g. to compute performance metrics of queues or QNs with low service rates more time is needed than for those with high service rates. This does not apply to the calculation by the analytical formulas. The Markovian Queue Solver takes longer the larger the number of servers in a node is, the higher the finite capacity is and the higher the population size is. But the necessary time for computation is independent of the service rates. On the whole, comparisons have clearly confirmed that the time savings of the analytical method are much bigger than those of the simulation, even for small QNs or single queues.

7. Conclusion

This paper consists of two main parts. The thirst part deals with basic queueing theory and how performance metrics of a resource / queue can be determined by an analytical way. Following goal was set for this topic: Choose queueing models and automate the calculation of the average number of customers, the throughput, the utilization and the response time of them (cf. chapter 3). In the second part we consider systems of interconnected queues (Queueing Networks) and analyze if and how performance metrics of QNs can be solved by formulas of the basic queueing theory. Workload propagation is of central importance for that. Following goal was defined: Apply the base formulas on queues that are part of (selected) Queueing Network models. (cf. chapter 3).

To reach the first goal the Markovian Queue Solver was developed. The analytical solver has implemented formulas for the four mentioned performance metrics that were derived from the generalized system-level model. But not every resource is solvable with that tool. Queues must fulfil two characteristics to be solvable:

- the Markovian or memoryless assumption, which says that the system depends only on the current state defined by the number of requests in the system (as a result arrival and service rates are exponentially distributed)

- scheduling discipline: FCFS, LCFS, PS and IS

That kind of queues are the most used ones. The Markovian Queue Solver can be used for queue models that are open or closed, load independent (single server queues) as well as load dependent (multiple server queues) and capacity limitations are considered, too. Furthermore the solver can be extended for computing delay resources i.e. $M/M/\infty$ queues or $M/M/\infty/N$ queues (formulas can be derived from the generalized system-level model, some formulas of probabilities can alternatively be found in [GPN98]) and the average number of lost requests for queues with finite capacity (some formulas can be found in [MA98]).

Computed performance results of the Markovian Queue Solver were compared with simulation results (by JSIMGraph). In most cases the results were consistent with some minimal, negligible deviations under 5% (cf. chapter 6). But also large deviations in the following two cases have occurred:

- When the queue has a multiple server, the average utilization differs between the Markovian Queue Solver and JSIMGraph.

- All four performance metrics vary for closed models with limited capacity between the Markovian Queue Solver and JSIMGraph.

Reasons for the deviations are a different understanding/definition of the average utilization or the queueing model (see section 6.1 for more information). Therefore users should be aware of how the performance models and metrics are defined by a performance solver tools before working with them.

The next main focus was on Queueing Network models. Analyzed QNs consisted of resources, which are solvable with the Markovian Queue Solver (restrictions are mentioned above). They belong to the class of product-form QNs. A discussion of the possibility of solving performance measures by the implemented formulas was mostly conceptional. A practical evaluation of the results, which were obtained conceptionally, also took place. It has been shown that for open QN models workload can be propagated and therefore basic queueing formulas can be used to solve performance metrics. However for closed models the workload cannot be propagated easily and the use of the basic queueing formulas is very limited.

In open models workload propagation is possible because:

- arrival rates are fixed

- jobs arrive from an external source and leave the system after getting served, so there is a clear starting point for workload propagation and the workload of a queue i depends on the predecessor queues only

In closed models workload propagation is difficult because:

- arrival rates are variable

- a fix number of requests cycles in the system, so there is no starting point for workload propagation in equilibrium and workload of a queue i depends on all queues of the QN

Open QNs with routing probabilities and with more customer classes are solvable by the basic queueing formulas. QNs where customer classes switch after getting served were not considered, but workload propagation should also be possible there. In addition not only performance metrics of queues of the open QN can be calculated, but also the response time and the average number of requests of the complete system. The response time of the single nodes have to be summed up to get the system response time. Likewise the average number of requests of the single nodes have to be summed up to get the system average number of requests.

The interarrival rates of closed QNs could not be determined by the basic queueing formulas. And even if the interarrival rates would be known, the performance metrics of the bottleneck queue is not solvable by the basic formulas. Therefore it is not recommended to use the Markovian Queue Solver for closed QNs. But there are good alternative analytical possibilities like the MVA algorithm for closed product-form QNs (cf. section 5.2.2). Furthermore there are techniques to reduce closed QNs.

Another part of this paper, which relates to QNs, is a practical comparison of the analytical Solver (Markovian Queue Solver) and a simulation (cf. chapter 6). For analytical processes more restrictions are necessary than for simulation processes. Nevertheless the application of the basic queueing formulas to a simulation method has advantages. Simulation tools could get problems (because of overflow) when they compute performance metrics of QNs, where the arrival rate of at least one node is bigger than the service rate. With the analytical approach workload can be propagated and therefore some queues of the QNs can be solved (where the arrival rate is smaller than the service rate). But the biggest advantage is the savings in computational costs. When we tested simple open QN models, in which nodes were interconnected in series, the analytical method (propagate workload for all nodes and use implemented formulas of the Markovian Queue Solver) was 108 to 243 times faster (cf. figure 7.1 and section 6.3)! Even for small systems (e.g. one queue) the Markovian Queue Solver was 27 to 47 times faster than JSIMGraph (cf. section 6.3).

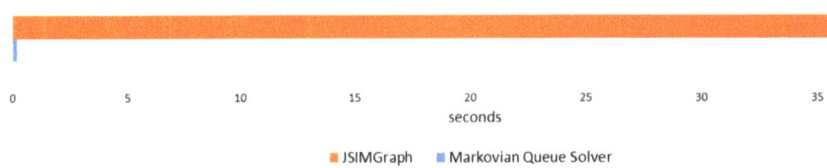

Figure 7.1: Required time for solving performance metrics of a tandem QN with ten nodes

This bachelor thesis shows the potential of analytical solving procedures, since results can be calculated much faster than by a simulation. Many different models can be compared quickly. An analytical solver can be used to search for specific parameter values in an approximate manner (e.g. which service rate is necessary to get an average utilization of 70%?). Furthermore there are techniques to reduce large systems (cf. FES algorithm of section 5.2.2). However, it has become clear that analytical procedures involve more restrictions than simulation tools.

Future work / possibilities:

- Markovian Queue Solver can be extended for delay resources and for calculation of average lost requests for queues with capacity limitations.

- A meta-model for QNs can be created, where the Markovian Queue Solver can be used or it can be connected to an existing meta-model like the JSIM-meta model.

- The Markovian Queue Solver can be used to search for specific parameter values in an approximate manner for closed Queueing Network models.

- Further algorithms can be considered and implemented especially to compute performance measures of closed Queueing Networks.

Bibliography

[Bal00]   S. Balsamo, "Product form queueing networks," in *Performance Evaluation: Origins and Directions.* Springer, 2000, pp. 377–401.

[BGdMT98] G. Bolch, S. Greiner, H. de Meer, and K. S. Trivedi, *Queueing networks and Markov chains: modeling and performance evaluation with computer science applications.* John Wiley & Sons, 1998.

[GPN98]   E. Gelenbe, G. Pujolle, and J. Nelson, *Introduction to queueing networks.* Wiley New York, 1998.

[Jai90]   R. Jain, *The art of computer systems performance analysis: techniques for experimental design, measurement, simulation, and modeling.* John Wiley & Sons, 1990.

[JMT]   "Java modelling tools." [Online]. Available: http://jmt.sourceforge.net/

[Kou05]   S. Kounev, *Performance Engineering of Distributed Component-Based Systems - Benchmarking, Modeling and Performance Prediction.* Shaker Verlag, Ph.D. Thesis, Technische Universität Darmstadt, Germany, December 2005, best Dissertation Award from the "Vereinigung von Freunden der Technischen Universität zu Darmstadt e.V.". [Online]. Available: http://www.amazon.de/exec/obidos/ASIN/3832247130/302-7474121-6584807

[MA98]   D. A. Menasce and V. Almeida, *Capacity Planning for Web Services: metrics, models, and methods.* Prentice Hall PTR, 1998.

[MADD04]   D. A. Menasce, V. A. Almeida, L. W. Dowdy, and L. Dowdy, *Performance by design: computer capacity planning by example.* Prentice Hall Professional, 2004.

[Ste09]   W. J. Stewart, *Probability, Markov chains, queues, and simulation: the mathematical basis of performance modeling.* Princeton University Press, 2009.

8. Appendix

VBA Visual Basic for Applications

CCNC Coalesce Computation of Normalizing Constants

CPU Central Processing Unit

DAC Distribution Analysis by Chain

FES Flow Equivalent Server

Java Java Programming Language

JMT Java Modeling Tools

LBANC Local Balance Algorithm for Normalizing constants

MVA Mean Value Analysis

QN Queueing Network

Recal Recursion by Chain Algorithm

YOUR KNOWLEDGE HAS VALUE

- We will publish your bachelor's and master's thesis, essays and papers

- Your own eBook and book -
  sold worldwide in all relevant shops

- Earn money with each sale

Upload your text at www.GRIN.com
and publish for free